For Gerard Galvin

Poet of the plate and the page

With thanks to:

Myrtle Allen, Pascal Bradley, Francis Brennan, Denis Cotter,

John Desmond, Gerard Galvin, Yoichi Hoashi,

Eugene McSweeney, Liz Mee, Helen Mullane & Armel Whyte,

Alan O'Reilly, Bernadette O'Shea and Nick Price,

for their testimonies

and

Gary Joyce, Nick Cann, Andrew McElroy, Chris Carroll,

Sally, Connie, Sam and Patrick

● John McKenna was born in Belfast, and educated there and in Dublin, where he studied law at University College, Dublin, and The Honorable Society of Kings Inns. He practised at the Bar before turning to writing full time.

● In 1989 John and Sally McKenna produced the first Irish Food Guide, and since 1991 have produced the series of guides to Ireland's food culture known collectively as the Bridgestone Guides.

● Their unique approach to exploring the complete food culture has won the guides international acclaim, and they are established as the leading guides to Ireland's food culture.

● John and Sally McKenna won the first André Simon Special Award for the 1991 Bridgestone Irish Food Guide, and the 1993 edition of The Bridgestone Irish Food Guide was short-listed for a Glenfiddich Award.

● John McKenna has won three Glenfiddich awards as a writer and broadcaster, as Restaurant Writer, Regional Writer and for Radio Programme of the Year.

● John McKenna writes on food for The Irish Times, and contributes to many newspapers and magazines worldwide.

CONTENTS

INTRODUCTION

The fundamental premise of this book is that restaurants are an entertainment, and beginning from this basic principle I have tried to examine how this entertainment works, and how, if you understand the principles underlying the entertainment, you have a better chance of running a restaurant which will be successful.

There are plenty of books which attempt to instruct people in the business of running a restaurant, and they usually take the approach of suggesting that you should ensure you have a good solicitor, and a reputable plumber, and go to a decent employment agency to recruit your staff. All of that knowledge is presumed in this book, and if you don't already know the nuts and bolts of getting a business started, then I would suggest you should abandon any ambitions for running a restaurant immediately, because you will not succeed without these basic requirements.

This book begins, then, at that point when the basic actions have begun, and explores what one needs to do to open a successful restaurant. It is true that there are restaurants where the primary function is simply to feed people, but for the most part people go to restaurants to be entertained, and in this context the food is only one element of the entertainment. Modern restaurant history suggests that a restaurateur needs to have a huge battery of skills in order to be successful, and this book attempts to describe what those necessary skills are, and how they should be deployed in order to create a place which people enjoy. It may seem somewhat ironic to have a person whose primary role is that of a restaurant critic writing a book about how to successfully run a restaurant. It might be worthwhile to explain, then, that my

INTRODUCTION

childhood was spent helping out in the family pub, and my adolescence and student years were spent washing dishes in numerous restaurants and, for one forlorn period, a year spent bashing out burgers in a fast food outlet. I have seen the business from the other side of the swing doors, and have tried to bring an appreciation of the dynamics and mechanics of the industry to play in my role as a critic.

I dislike the idea of the critic who pronounces on restaurant dishes from on high, and who seems only able to pay attention to their personal preferences. In all of my writing on food, what I have tried to examine is the idea of a food culture, and to reveal the connections between producers, suppliers and cooks and then, finally, how this food chain ends within the context of the entertainment of the restaurant.

It is a fact that all restaurateurs must understand, that the better one understands this idea of the food chain, then the better you are equipped to run a successful restaurant. Indeed, every successful restaurant is, in its own terms, a complete culture, embracing relations with suppliers, staff, customers and critics. All human life is encompassed within the brilliant, beautiful dynamic and choreography of a restaurant, and there is the possibility for instinctive creativity and artistry to be expressed and demonstrated.

I frequently liken the running of a good restaurant to the operation of a stage show: the idea, the concept, the cast, the script written and endlessly amended until it is right, the rehearsal, the ambition, the desire to please, the preparation, the lighting, the music, then the performance and the response of the audience, finally the satisfaction of a good evening's entertainment. It is this part of the business which this book explores, and it is a part of the industry which has been largely ignored by the schools and colleges which educate students in the business.

But this book is not merely for students. The most successful restaurateurs, it seems to me, are people who never stay still. They are constantly on the lookout for ways in which to improve what they do, and in my experience their restless striving usually brings even more success. For it also seems to me to be obvious that if one is successful in the restaurant trade, then it encourages people to stay put, and to do the same old thing each and every day. You cannot do this any longer, for there is too much competition in the business these days, and too much hunger on the part of customers to explore the new and innovative. Practitioners, then, must continually examine what they are doing, and ask themselves if it could be done better, if they could be finding a way to attract and satisfy more and more people.

This drive is also necessary in order to satisfy staff, and to unleash their creative potential. For creativity is the keynote to being a successful restaurateur. The kitchen which loses its creative focus, the staff who simply go through the motions, the entertainment which is nothing more than a rerun through the same old tricks, is not the sort of place to which the modern customer, who has the money which allows him to be very choosy, will want to return. Every time you open the doors, the entertainment must be made anew.

JOHN MCKENNA
DURRUS, COUNTY CORK

THE ACTION

There is no mystery as to why people want to run restaurants and why people want to eat in them.
A restaurant running at full speed, with the staff engaged, the customers happy, the atmosphere bristling, the food flowing seamlessly from kitchen to table, is a beautiful sight, a sublime enchantment, for all concerned.

Restaurants are beautiful, restaurants are sublime

The extraordinary synchronicity involved, the painstaking detail required of every action, the magnificent choreography operating between staff and customers, creates one of the most fascinating, pleasureful and inspiring inventions of our society.

Little else in our daily lives is so intense, so direct. Above all, little else in our daily lives is so directly devoted to giving pleasure. Because that is what restaurants are all about: pleasure. Even the simplest thing prepared in a restaurant will at least attempt to give the customer pleasure, will help them to feel good, simply by the fact that the food is prepared to be shared, the fact that someone had made the effort to make something for you.

And, at its very best, a restaurant can give more fun, more amusement, more direct engagement with the senses than anything else. The cinema is fine, but its very nature keeps us at a distance, and the spectacle is pre-ordained: it cannot be altered. The theatre is a re-enactment. A concert comes closest to the spontaneity of an evening in a restaurant, but again there is inevitably some distance between us and the performers.

But an evening in a restaurant pitches us head first into contact with all the artistic values we cherish. The creativity and volatility of the cook. The engagement and personality of the waiter. The creation and appreciation of the atmosphere and the ambience. The succour and satisfaction of the food. The allurement and beguilement of the wine. Only jazz music, with its emphasis on improvisation, gets close to the wild creativity of a restaurant working at its best.

Above all, a restaurant, working at its best, is a place of mass seduction, nothing less. And a place of immediate, happening artistry. Art in Action. That is what restaurants do, and the fact that the art work is consumed, and thereby destroyed, makes them even more valuable. For their art is ephemeral, and thus more intense, because it is not self conscious, as so much art is, and it is less dictated to by the medium. Most theatre needs a stage, most music likewise, cinema needs a projector. But a restaurant can supply something sublime with only the very simplest tools and space. The perfect sandwich, artfully prepared, in a roadside stop. A piece of char-grilled fish on a patio. A painter may need only a piece of paper and some charcoal to prepare the most intense, perfect sketch, and the cook can do just the same, and create something just as perfect.

A SINGLE FRYING PAN IS THE FOUNDATION OF EVERY GREAT RESTAURANT,

along with a hob, a plate and a table. Everything else is decoration.

There are lots of theories which suggest that people go to restaurants as a form of self-reward, to pay themselves back for some achievement in their lives. Perhaps this is the case, and certainly many people still make the mistake of only going to restaurants for special occasions: the 40th birthday, the exam passed, the promotion achieved.

But modern restaurant eating is not as simple as that. People need to eat, people need to be fed, of course, and people cook less and less at home. But it is not fanciful to suggest that what people are searching for when they go into a restaurant is the very engagement with other people and with other peoples' creativity which can be so difficult to achieve elsewhere.

Our lives are increasingly conducted at a distance from direct human contact in many areas. But if we sit down in a restaurant – providing it is not just a fast food stop or some other form of automated food production which has no place in a book like this – then various people have to perform a complex, and directly involving, series of actions for us. We might take it for granted, because it seems so obvious, but the meeting and greeting is the first thing we want, and then the offer of a drink, even just the simple act of placing a jug of water on the table, but most delightfully the pop of a cork as it is pulled from a bottle.

Then we consider and contemplate, and our order is taken. And then we know that someone is preparing our food, just as someone has prepared the table and someone has prepared the atmosphere by selecting the music and the paintings and the decor and the furniture. And then – one of the key actions – the food is brought to us, for our enjoyment, and we chat and eat and drink and relax, and the food consoles and pleases us, and the wine increases the pleasure, and we are grateful for the entire brilliant, complex machinery and the intense spontaneity of the restaurant, that choreography of human talents which makes it all possible.

It does not matter if we are ordering a sandwich and a cup of tea, or truffled lobster, followed by a burnt orange custard for dessert. All food service, properly done, shares the capacity and the potential to create pleasure, providing it is done with a generous heart, thereby revealing the care of the cook and the staff, and their desire to delight and impress the customer.

For the fundamental rule of food, the rule which underpins everything in this book, is that food cooked with care is good food, and food cooked by rote, even should it be foie gras and lobster, is bad food. The smartest restaurant can produce the most depressing experience, simply because we can sense that all they want, deep down, is our cash.

But the simplest little place, maybe making no more than bread rolls and sandwiches, but where we sense that the people are committed to doing their best, fires us with excitement and delight, because we are seeing human creativity and commitment in action. That is why people love good food, and why every cook and restaurateur has a duty to be engaged and committed to doing their best. Restaurants are only beautiful, restaurants are only sublime, when they are places where the cook and the staff care about the customer. Otherwise, they are just feeding houses.

You have to love it, or else forget it

The testimonies of the restaurateurs quoted in this book all show that running a restaurant is one of the hardest things you can choose to do. In fact, a good restaurateur is the closest we can get to defining a modern renaissance man or woman. They must be fluent in countless disciplines: cookery, design, service, staff management, efficiency, hygiene, fashion, music. And, after you have mastered all that, you get to sit down and do the VAT.

If you don't love the whole business of restaurants, the whole wonderful catharsis of cooking and caring for your customers, then you will never hack it in the business, and you should never consider going into the business at all. Restaurant life is anti-social, for the restaurateur. Everyone else's holiday is your busiest time at work. Everyone else will be out at 8pm on a Friday night. So will you. But you will be working and they will be relaxing.

So why do people do it, especially considering that few of them will make very much money doing it? The answer is simple. Just as customers love the romance and enchantment of a good restaurant, so do restaurateurs. It is their canvas, remember. It is their performance space. And they are performers, first and foremost.

IT IS NOT A BUSINESS. IT IS A VOCATION.
ABOVE ALL, IT IS A PASSION.

And what do they get for it, if not money? The answer is the regard, applause and respect of their customers, their public. And that response and regard is almost instantaneous. A painter may sell a painting to a client and few people will, thereafter, see the work. But a restaurateur, a chef, is giving pleasure to many people each and every time they tie on the apron, fire up the stove, set the tables and open the doors.

People love good food much more than they love good books, good movies or good paintings, and if you are the person responsible for giving them that good food in a beautiful space, then they will respect you much more than they respect any author, director or painter. Restaurateurs are addicted to this regard, addicted to the acclaim of their public. And that is why they do it, and that is why they are determined to do it well every single time. It is not a business. It is a vocation. Above all, it is a passion.

The republic of pleasure

Every good restaurant experience begins with the greeting, and if the greeting is wrong, then the experience is off to the worst possible start. To understand why the greeting is so important, we need to look at what the customer wants when they walk through the door.

Of course, they may be doing nothing more than grabbing a sandwich off the shelf and asking you for a bottle of mineral water before they rush back to the office. If that is the case, then you need to understand that they don't want to be engaged in conversation. They will respect you if you can read and appreciate that, and serve them as briskly and competently as possible. If you do that, they will come back.

But if it is Friday evening, after a long week, and a group of friends or family walk though the door of the restaurant, then what do they want? The answer is simple: they want to be transported into a little republic of pleasure, where everyday concerns and pressures are absent. They want you to take them to that little republic of pleasure, and

THE ACTION

you begin the journey by doing the very simplest thing: greeting them. "Hello, good evening and welcome" is the most clichéd of greetings, made famous by David Frost on his many television programmes, but it is not the correct one.

"Hello, good evening, you're welcome" may not sound very different, but it is crucially different. By saying "You're welcome", you single out the passengers who you are going to take with you, you make them feel special. You must make every customer feel that their individual needs are paramount: it is *you* who are welcome.

Those people who are masters of the art manage this, seemingly effortlessly. But it is not effortless, it is their genius, even if they say it to 400 people each night.

The genius understands, then, that the key language at this time is all propositional, and this brings us to back to appreciating that the customer wants to surrender control of the evening, but only under their own terms.

SO YOU DO NOT DIRECT, YOU PROPOSE: it is no accident that the French use this language: *Je vous propose.*

And so you say: "May I show you to a table?" May I take your coat?" "Would you like something to drink? An aperitif, a kir?" Remember, also, that many people are slightly nervous on entering a restaurant, so a series of propositions is elemental to putting them at their ease, especially the direct suggestion of a particular drink: a kir, a glass of prosecco, even a glass of champagne if you understand that the occasion is a special one. The propositional language absolves them of responsibility, asserts your authority and your care, and gets everything off to a flying start.

The sacramental sharing

There is one other key action at this point, and if it is the simplest thing, it is also the most elemental, and vital. Bread and water should be placed on the table. Even though the overall transaction is, fundamentally, a commercial one – you are selling food and wine and they are paying for it – you should never lose sight of the sacramental element of eating and drinking. They are going to share food amongst themselves, and there is a sacramental factor in this, no matter how simple the food and the circumstances. By offering the most elemental of foods – bread and water – we acknowledge that sacramental sharing.

If all you ever do is to sell these foods, you are making a mistake. They don't need to eat the bread, and they may prefer to order and to pay for bottled water. It doesn't matter, that is their choice. By placing the bread and water on the table you are making one of the most profound statements about the entire act of eating and drinking, and even if the customers appear not to acknowledge it, it will nevertheless reverberate in their subconscious. It is your offer, your invitation and, following it, everything can now begin.

The theatre of the restaurant

Life is not a stage, but restaurants are. One of the main attractions for a customer is not merely the food served in a restaurant, but the entire theatre of the evening: the sparkle, the atmosphere, the bustle and hubbub, the music, the setting, the service and, then, the integration of suitable food into the right ambience and setting. Restaurants are inherently dramatic, and that is why people are attracted to them.

So many elements are involved in serving food to customers that the drama is omnipresent, and restaurateurs should never overlook the importance of considering their work as a performance.

I was struck recently, when reading an interview with one of the most successful and admired Dublin chefs and restaurateurs, when the chef admitted that driving in to his restaurant for evening service his stomach muscles would be tied up in knots, due to the tension and pressure of the work, the defining desire to make everything perfect.

THE ACTION

This is, of course, the equivalent of stage fright, often thought to be the exclusive preserve of actors and musicians. But chefs and waiters are also performers, and need to understand that. Your stomach muscles should be tied in knots: it goes with the job.

THEY ALSO NEED, THEN, TO APPRECIATE THAT THEY MUST NOT OVERACT. There is nothing so calculated to alienate a customer as a stagy waiter, who performs everything in a camp theatricality, right from the first greeting to the final flourish as they peer over your shoulder to see what sort of tip your are signing onto the credit card slip.

The key thing here, as so often, is to read the customer. The young couple in the first throes of passion want to be left well alone. The party crowd on a Friday night will not merely enjoy your witticisms, they will tip you for them at the end of the evening. The business suits want you to make sure everything is seamless, and then to let them get on with the subtleties of their business strategies. The middle-aged couple want some general chat and some hints and advice about the food and wine, and want to be involved in the goings-on of the restaurant more than anyone else, particularly if they are regular customers.

It is the greatest cliché of them all, of course, to say that the best waiters are simply themselves, but it is a cliché because it is true. Once the waiter has mastered the nuts and bolts of food service, then the vital signal they impart to the customer is confidence, and that confidence is what puts the customer at their ease.

To draw an analogy with the stage, a waiter must be a sort of Method Actor: you study and analyse everything, all the better to hide it in your performance, and to make it seem as natural as possible. Of course it isn't natural, and the customer knows that, but we are playing with illusions here, we are on stage, in performance.

The element of theatre, then, invades every detail of the production. The stage must be dressed and lit before the performance can take place. The costumes must be considered. There must be a script, and there must be a director and actors and, above all, there must be a vision.

THE VISION THING

It might seem remarkable to suggest that some people go through the entire complex, expensive and tortuous rigmarole of setting up a restaurant and not really have a clear idea as to why they are doing it, but it is often the case. And, if that does happen, the one thing you can be sure of is that the restaurant will fail. You need to be able to give a very definite answer to these questions:

WHY AM I DOING THIS?

WHAT DO I WANT TO ACHIEVE?

WHAT DO I WANT TO OFFER PEOPLE?

WHAT REWARD OR SATISFACTIONS WILL I GET FOR DOING IT?

THE VISION THING

Why are you doing it?

Because you love the glamour and the theatricality and the sheer excitement of cooking and running a restaurant and it gives you a chance to express yourself, as we have said before. If you don't like all these things, above all if you simply think it might be a nice idea, or you just want to impress people, then forget it. You are doomed to fail.

What do I want to achieve?

Satisfaction, and the pleasure of a job well done, basically. Cooking and service are art forms, and provide the satisfaction which any artist derives from their work. Of course there are headaches, countless headaches and frustrations, but there are headaches and frustrations in every occupation.

What do I want to offer people?

This is one of the most vital considerations, and the answer is that you want to offer them something which makes you happy. In other words, if you are a meticulous, talented cook with an exacting technique, then you will not be happy with simple, short-order cooking, because it will give you no opportunity to express yourself. If you want to offer people a slice of the cutting-edge, then that is what you have to plan your restaurant around; the food is the key element, with everything else supporting it.

But if you are not a cutting edge cook, then look again at why you are in the restaurant business. Do you simply want to create a congenial place where people can enjoy good food and have a good time? If so, then don't for a second imagine that this is a less exalted calling than being at the cutting edge. It isn't. The critical theory that only cutting edge, highly technical cookery is worthy of acclaim is nonsense. The cook who makes a perfect sandwich is as much of an artist as the driven chef with his towering, involved cooking ascending up from the plate. Society needs different types of food in different types of places for a multitude of different reasons.

The answer to the question, then, is that what you want to offer people is a bit of yourself, your tastes, your passions, your preoccupations, your preferences. The great Belfast restaurateur, Nick Price, always jokes that running a restaurant is simply a chance to inflict your taste on other people. Mr Price makes a joke out of it, but it is absolutely true. The restaurant that gives its chef and its staff a chance to express themselves is a happy place. The formal restaurant where everything is buttoned down to a formula is not a happy place – just go to any high-roller French restaurant and see if the people are having a good time. They aren't.

The inspirational Californian restaurateur, Alice Waters, has written that she opened Chez Panisse, her legendary Berkeley restaurant, because "all I cared about was a place to sit down with my friends and enjoy good food whilst discussing the politics of the day. And I believed that in order to experience food as good as I had in France, I had to cook it myself'". A restaurateur was born.

What rewards and satisfactions will I get?

Well, if you run a decent restaurant, you will make a decent living from working very long hours. You won't make as much as a bank manager, or a television executive. But you will do okay. Unless you get very lucky, and stumble into a media career or something like that, you will not get rich. Not a chance. In this regard, you will be like most artists. A few musicians and painters and writers get lucky and get rich, but only a few. Most simply work away doing what they do, and live for the pleasure of a job well done, a job that manages to pay the rent.

The reward and satisfactions of running a successful restaurant are often intangible things. Is there really pleasure to be had from running a busy place on a crazy night, when at the end of it all you are utterly exhausted? Of course there is. It is the pleasure of creating and serving good food, and thereby creating happiness. It is the pleasure of being truly engaged, with food, with people, with a vibrant social life. Few jobs actually offer comparable pleasures, offer comparable spontaneity and excitement.

So, the vision thing means taking a long hard look, at yourself. Because if the vision is not yours, and thereby shared by your team and, then, your customers, you will fail. You might still manage to run a fairly successful restaurant, but there will be no pleasure in it, at least not for yourself.

Never copy anyone

Every successful restaurant creates its own dynamic, and that dynamic creates its success. As such, every successful restaurant contains its own original idea. The restaurant may adapt the approach and formula of another place, but without its own jot of inspiration, it simply will not succeed. And the reason why it will not succeed is simple: people hate a fake, and they can spot one miles off.

Most people who go to restaurants regularly are sophisticated, and eager to be surprised and delighted. If they walk into your room and the decor and style is a copy of someone elses, and they open the menu and say "But this is the same sort of food as they serve at Wittgenstein's, up the road!", then you are doomed. They will compare you to Wittgenstein's, and almost certainly compare you badly, simply because people hate those who copy.

This is one reason why bourgeois restaurants are so monotonous. They copy a high-roller formula – big glasses, big paintings, formal service, French-influenced cooking, white linen – and the boring thing is that it has all been done before. The most important thing seems to be the amount of money which has been spent, and the belief that this is what people want. It isn't.

People don't look at sumptuous furnishing and big paintings and say:

"How wonderful. This must be a good place". Instead, it makes them suspicious. What they really say is: "These guys are going to be charging me too much for the food, because how else are they going to get their money back?". Adopt a formula, and you have already begun to alienate the customer.

So, you can adapt and refine an idea which comes from someone else, but above all there must be something of you, something original, in how you design the restaurant and how you write your menu. And the originality must not be gratuitous. If you decide to serve all your wines by the bucket, just because it is novel, you won't have people thanking you for it. They will just think you are stupid, and go eat someplace else.

A REFINEMENT OF ANY IDEA MUST PURSUE ITS LOGIC,

or else it won't work. If you want to run an informal, city-centre place with a high turnover, where people eat informal food pretty quickly, then you need to look very seriously at the key questions for an operation of this nature: service, value, efficiency.

If, on the other hand, you want to run a place with six tables, three rooms upstairs and you want to close for the winter each year and chill out, then the questions you have to explore are wholly different. What you need to be concerned about now is uniqueness, creativity and character, because these are the elements which will bring people to your restaurant, irrespective of the distance they might have to travel, and if you don't have them in place, then the concept won't work. You need, in however small a measure, to offer people something which is different and novel, but which is still entirely logical within the context of the sort of place you want to run.

Location, location, location

Let's explore this idea further by invoking the mantra of the restaurateur Peter Langan, who famously replied to a question that the three most

THE VISION THING

important ingredients for a successful restaurant were "Location, location and location".

Peter Langan was right, of course. In a city, location of a restaurant is vital to success, especially if you run the sort of place Peter Langan did, an expensive, formal restaurant which is serviced by the guests of nearby expensive hotels.

And Peter Langan was also wrong, because location can play an entirely different role in the success of a restaurant. Instead of being at the centre of things, you can have a location which is at the extremity, and it will, paradoxically, be an element of your success.

John Desmond and Ellmary Fenton run Island Cottage Restaurant on Heir Island, a small island off the coast of South-West Cork. To get to the restaurant, you must take a ferry boat, from a variety of locations. You must then walk about half a mile along a boreen to get to the house. The restaurant is a single room. There is no choice on the menu. The only staff are John, who cooks, and Ellmary, who takes care of front of house. It is as unlikely a set-up as one could imagine, a million miles away from Peter Langan's slick, city-centre hustle and bustle.

And Island Cottage is also one of the great modern Irish restaurants, hugely successful during its short season each year, and it is not an exaggeration to say that its remoteness and its unlikeliness are one of the reasons for its success. The location does play a part, simply because it is so strange and inspired, so challenging. Its awkwardness is, truly, a virtue. Island Cottage Restaurant takes Peter Langan's dictum, and turns it on its head.

So the rule here is simple. The rule for success is to break the rules. Not all the rules, but at least some of them, enough to make your restaurant special. If you want a restaurant in the city, you should observe the mantra that location is vital, and then reconfigure your formula to make it special. Away from the city, you can do what you like, for the clientele is wholly different, and the more of a challenge you offer them, the better.

THE UNBENDING RULE

You can break just about every rule in the restaurant business and, if you do it properly, your lawlessness will help you to succeed.
But there is one unbending rule which cannot be broken, and it is this:

BE CONSISTENT

PEOPLE LOVE BRILLIANCE, but deep down they actually prefer certainty.

If they are going to spend their money in your restaurant, they want the assurance that this time, everything will be just as good as the last time. If you cannot guarantee them that this will be the case, the chances are that they will go someplace else. The most successful restaurants are, above all else, consistent, with consistently high standards within their own realm. If the spicy chicken wings you eat with your fingers are good every time, you will never tire of eating them. If the lobster thermidor you eat with fine cutlery is good every time, you will never tire of eating it.

But if the standard slips, then the customer's confidence in you will be eroded, because people only ever tire of bad food. If your cooking is complex and, thereby, offers more chances of things going wrong, then you are playing a risky game indeed. The chef who understands how a dish can be achieved consistently every time is the smart cook. The genius who improvises endlessly is less likely to be a successful restaurateur, no matter how thrilling and inspiring his work is.

THE UNBENDING RULE

Be simple

Escoffier, whose cooking was often absurdly complex, was the man who said

"Faites simple" and thereby bequeathed one of the most confusing dictums to the restaurant world.

What did he mean, the chef whose recipe for Fillets of Sole Olga involves cooking and then hollowing out potatoes, filling them with shelled prawns mixed with a little Sauce Vin Blanc on top of which a fillet of sole which has been poached in stock is placed, and atop which you place some sauce Mornay before a final sprinkling of Parmesan announces that the dish is ready to be gratinated in a very hot oven. That is keeping it simple?

I THINK WHAT ESCOFFIER MEANT WAS "BE LOGICAL".

If you are cooking and serving complex food, then you must observe the logic which will make the dish work, however involved it may be. If you are making a sandwich, the same rule applies. In short, there must be nothing gratuitous in a dish, nothing which is there simply for effect, nothing which does not contribute to the flavour and, thereby, the satisfaction, of the dish.

You might think, for example, that a festoon of saffron strands makes a mighty attractive decoration for a dish, perhaps sitting high atop a fish dish. But it isn't a good idea, because strands of saffron are not edible, and the customer who knows this will simply push them to the side of the plate, curse the expensive waste, and think you are an idiot. This logic is neglected to the greatest cost in the modern fashion for fusion cooking. You cannot simply combine a variety of chopped foods with a bunch of coriander, toss it into a wok, and hope it will work. It won't.

Good fusion cooking is as rigorously logical as any other style of cooking, and what a good restaurateur is always hunting for are flavours which are complementary and appropriate.

RULE ONE IS: if it ain't broke, don't fix it. Cook your sole on the bone for flavour. Beef loves béarnaise. Fish loves hollandaise. Potatoes like persillade, and so do mushrooms. These are immutable laws.

RULE TWO IS: if you are going to fix it, then only add in those things which will work. If you want to make a sabayon for your oysters Rockefeller, then use Guinness for the sauce, because oysters like Guinness. If you are making your Dublin coddle with shellfish instead of pork, make sure the various fish combine as efficiently as the classic pairing of rashers and sausages and onions. You abandon the logic of flavour at your peril. Always be led by the ingredients you are using, and their needs and preferences.

Perfect is perfect

Another consideration which the restaurateur and chef should be aware of is this: if a piece of good beef and a dish of fine organic spuds are perfect – and the best beef and the best spuds will be perfect – then adding some sliced truffle won't make the dish more perfect, and serving it on fine Wedgewood, or on a starched linen tablecloth, won't make it more perfect either.

LESS IS MORE WHEN IT COMES TO GOOD COOKING, simply because it concentrates the mind of the customer on what they are eating. If too much is going on on the plate, the chances of achieving perfection are reduced. Elaboration should never be so involved that it loses track of the essential tastes and shape of the food.

ELABORATION IS NOT SOPHISTICATION, and for some customers it creates suspicion regarding the basic quality of the food. A chervil leaf, placed in the right way, may be all the elaboration which a dish needs.

THE UNBENDING RULE

There is more to this statement of simplicity, of course, and I would suggest that it amounts to a revolutionary manifesto regarding the very idea of "perfection".

Previously, a critical consensus argued that the grander the establishment, the more it was worthy of attention, and the more involved the food was meant that it was more "serious", more worthy of attention. I think this is nonsense.

Perfection, I would argue, is the achievement of the ultimate of an individual's ability. Perfection is not enhanced by deep pile carpets, colossal glasses and bow tied waiters. A critic should judge an establishment and a meal in the context of how well it achieves what the individual set out to achieve.

If the chef says: "I have the best beef, and vegetables from my garden, and that is what I am going to cook", then so long as the chef hangs and prepares the meat properly, cooks it to your specification, captures the flavours of the individual vegetables and presents the dish with grace and care, then he has achieved perfection. All the other stuff is an irrelevance. Great domestic cooking has understood this for centuries. And so have the wisest, most creative restaurateurs throughout the world. We enjoy the irrelevances, of course, for they are part of the entertainment. But the core of great cooking, wherever it takes place, is focused on the perfection of ingredients.

THE SEARCH FOR PERFECTION BEGINS WITH THE HUNT FOR THE BEST INGREDIENT. Once that has been found – the best mountain lamb, the best meadow-grazed beef, the freshest fish and shellfish, organically-grown vegetables – then the job of the chef is to secure and capture the inherent flavours of the food. The possibility for perfection already exists within the ingredients, and the modern, smart chef understands that his job is simply to present those flavours for the customer.

If you do this, then you not only achieve perfection, but you also respect the logic of the food, and you secure the essential simplicity which makes food noble. That is what cooking is all about. Curnonsky, the great writer and explorer of regional foods, captured the concept in two stunning aphorisms:

"IN COOKING, AS IN ALL THE ARTS, SIMPLICITY IS THE SIGN OF PERFECTION"

"LA CUISINE! THAT'S WHEN THINGS TASTE LIKE THEMSELVES"

But we must add a note of caution to this exuberance, and quote one of modern cooking's great masters, Richard Olney, who, musing on the subject of simplicity in cooking, once wrote that:

"SIMPLICITY – NO DOUBT – IS A COMPLEX THING"

WHAT'S FOR DINNER?

It is not merely the customer who asks this question, it should also be the chef, asking of himself: what do I want to cook?

There are many restaurants which claim to succeed because "they give the customer what the customer wants". This is generally meant to understand that middle-market places can get away with serving big hunks of meat and plenty of dithery vegetables to people who don't much care what they are eating in the first place. These establishments will insist that their customers are "happy". No they are not; they are merely uninterested, and rather bored, just as the kitchen will be bored to tears cooking the same dishes, and the management will be bored to tears, for there will not be a single challenge in any aspect of their work.

You can sit down in these establishments, and you don't even need to open the menu to know what kind of food they will be offering: dull, unsophisticated, old-fashioned. They are dinosaurs, these places, and they are headed for extinction, for the modern eater thrives by challenge and surprise. Offer them these ingredients, and you will succeed. Which brings us back to the very idea of the restaurant in the first place: what should you cook? Let's explore this question by saying what you should not cook.

Don't cook what you don't understand

It sounds obvious, but the world is full of places where people have spotted a gap in the market – "There's no Tex-Mex-Fusion joint in town. Let's open one" – and then set about concocting a menu which owes something to the idea of the cuisine, but owes nothing whatsoever to the integrity and culture of the cuisine. These places produce the very worst food imaginable, simply because a commercially-driven approach owes nothing whatsoever to cuisine and the culture of cuisine. They can soldier on for a few years, producing poor food, and then they close, a fact which was always inevitable. A fake, commercial concept is not cooking.

Cook what you like to eat

Some people suggest that the very best women chefs succeed because they instinctively understand this key rule. Male chefs have egos and want to show off, but female chefs cook because they want to feed and please people. Their food is, thus, simpler, more logical, more enjoyable, and because it is often extremely personal, it is ultimately more successful.

Certainly, in Ireland, this is often the case with the leading female restaurateurs. I believe many of them do, intuitively, cook in this way, but it is not a form of culinary conservatism, it is simply cooking by instinct. They choose the foods which their palates understand from back-to-front, and because their olfactory systems are more sensitive than the male system, they never stray into silly improvisations which don't make culinary sense.

This is a contentious issue, and one could at any moment point out male cooks whose work is a celebration of instinct rather than technique. But it is certainly true that women tend, more than men, to cook and serve the food they themselves like to eat.

If this is the case, then I believe that they are right to do so.

"I opened a restaurant so that people could come and eat; remember that the final goal is to nourish and nurture those who gather at your table. It is there, within this nurturing process, that I have found the greatest satisfaction and sense of accomplishment"

Who else but the great Californian restaurateur, Alice Waters, would have written those words? The answer is that almost every female restaurateur could have written them.

WHAT'S FOR DINNER?

So, if you cook the food which is closest to your heart, the chances of it being true, and pure, and successful, are increased dramatically. To draw an analogy with painting, this implicit understanding of the medium will also, then, allow you to improvise with confidence. How can you personalise and improvise with foods and ingredients that you do not understand? You cannot. Let us return to Richard Olney's thoughts on the subject:

"The painter-cook analogy does not seem too far flung to me. There are many who believe that a healthy dose of imagination is all that one need bring to the kitchen. The cacophonous results are in quite the same spirit as the poignant failures of the liberated artist... Rules in cooking are not iron-cast (and, as in any medium of expression, they are often bent or broken by practitioners of talent – but to break rules, one must have rules)... One's own set of rules will form itself and become increasingly elaborate as one comes to understand the logic behind each detail, each step, to recognise the repetitions or variations of basic steps from one recipe to another; and the more elaborate the set of rules... the greater is the freedom lent one's creative imagination. Only a cookbook is needed to prepare a boeuf Bourguignon but, without rules, improvisation is impossible – and that is what cooking is all about"

Logic, rules, improvisation. That is what cooking is all about.

Tasting, tasting, tasting

No two prawns ever taste the same. No two fillets of beef ever taste the same. Summer tomatoes are completely different from tomatoes used in the winter which will have been imported. Kerry lamb has a different flavour from Wicklow lamb. Farmhouse cheeses vary radically in flavour depending on whether the milk used has been produced from grass or from silage. Granny Smith apples are wildly different in taste and texture from Cox's Pippins.

All of this is self-evident, and unarguable. But why, when cooks are forced to work with raw ingredients which are never the same twice, do so many of them behave as if recipes never need to be changed as the ingredients vary and differ? Why, in short, do so few cooks really taste the food they cook, all the while they are cooking it?

GOOD COOKING IS ALL ABOUT TASTING, TASTING, TASTING. If you have an ideal taste for a dish in your head, the only way you will achieve it is to continually taste the dish as it comes together, and keep adjusting and tuning the seasonings and the balance until you have the dish just right. The prawns you cooked on Tuesday night will be different from those you are cooking on Saturday night, so you must adapt and assimilate your flavours to achieve the ideal of taste. You must, then, improvise continually. Simply carrying out a recipe, and failing to appreciate how the flavours can vary from day to day, will not allow you to hit the peak of perfection which the dish demands. Taste, taste and taste again. Use your sense of touch to understand how well meat is cooked, how much more time it needs. Cooking is a hands-on business, and you should be eternally sticking your finger into sauces to taste them, and prodding meat to see if it is cooked just the way you want it to be. Don't hold back, don't be hands-off. Along with a sharp knife, every cook needs asbestos fingers, and it only takes a few scrapes and burns before you will have them.

WHAT'S FOR DINNER?

What should it look like?

If good cooking is when things taste of themselves, then good presentation occurs when food looks like itself. Simplicity of presentation is effective, because it follows the rule of culinary logic which is essential to successful cooking. The great Kerry restaurateur, Maura Foley, once succinctly described her culinary code to me as

"IN FOOD – SIMPLICITY",

and mused on the fact that an over-elaborate plate

"IS LIKE AN OVER-DRESSED WOMAN. OF COURSE I LOVE THE FLOURISH OF SOMETHING LIKE A PHILIP TREACY HAT, BUT NO MORE THAN THAT"

The great french chef, Pierre Koffman, uses a similar analogy:

"Comparing some of the more artificial exaggerations of nouvelle cuisine to the country cooking I knew as a boy always seems to me to be rather like dressing Marie Antoinette up as a shepherdess and then comparing her to a real farmer's wife looking after a real-life flock of sheep"

Koffmann is here discussing the core importance of regional cuisine in his own cooking, and how he simply takes and adapts techniques of the nouvelle cuisine and assimilates them into his work.

The similarity of the analogies is interesting, because what it reveals about two great cooks is their selectivity and vicious logic about their food, but also their articulate visual sense. Marie Antoinette will never look like a shepherdess: she will always look like a fake. An over-dressed woman will look absurd and incongruous, but a woman who is simply dressed, and who sports a Philip Treacy hat on her head, will show herself and the artful creativity of her hat to best effect.

WHAT'S FOR DINNER?

Overdressing is fatal, and trying to fake ingredients, to make them something they are not, is likewise doomed.

SO FOOD, THEN, SHOULD LOOK LIKE FOOD. It should be recognisable, and this applies to its colour as well as its appearance and, most definitely, its texture.

Decoration should be confined to garnishing, and here, also, the logic must not be lost.

The swirl of saffron threads atop the fillet of fish may look spectacular, but in fact it signifies an over-dressed plate, because the strands of saffron cannot be eaten, and so are a gratuitous gesture. A little sprig of chervil, in the place of the saffron, has culinary logic to it, not to mention grace and simplicity. We would not hesitate to suggest that an over-dressed person looks somewhat vulgar. Why are we so slow to say the same of an over-dressed plate? Because that is what it is: vulgar.

There is another reason why decoration should be kept simple: **HEAT**

Food which is elaborately piled on top of itself has much more chance of arriving at the table cold than a dish which goes straight from pan to warmed plate, is sauced and has some herbs placed atop, and is taken straight to the customer.

Heat is important in food, not just because it makes it more edible, but because as the dish cools it offers a changing series of temperatures and, thereby, textures. Food at the correct temperature – which is to say the temperature at which it is perfectly cooked – is more interesting to eat, whereas food which has to be re-heated to bring it to a temperature at which it can be brought to the table is losing some of its interest, along with its natural juices. The food, in fact, is being tortured when it is treated like this. The natural, logical flow of cooking – from raw to cooked to plate to table – is being disturbed, and food can only suffer when this is done.

TIMING IS EVERYTHING

Menu management

When you are running a restaurant, the choreography of all the players involved must be directed, and timing is everything.
Restaurants are run by the clock, and mastering the art of timing is crucial.

The best way to illustrate this is by looking at what the customer wants when they sit down. Bread and water, as we have already seen, and something to drink, served promptly, as this helps them to relax. This is a vital factor, for a nervous customer will be a difficult customer, whilst one who is relaxed will be much more patient, and much more fun to work with.

And, then, reasonably promptly, they want something to eat. Simple, isn't it? Yes it is, unless the restaurateur complicates it. And you can complicate it in this way: most people want to eat between 8pm and 8.30pm. If you accept all your bookings for this time, you will find that you go from an empty room to a full room in 30 minutes. Your kitchen will not be able to cope, simple as that.

If, then, you also make your choice of starters too complex – let us say that every starter actually has to be cooked and served hot – then your kitchen will collapse. The people in the door at 8pm will have food in

TIMING IS EVERYTHING

15 minutes, but the poor folk coming through at 8.30pm will still be waiting at 9.15pm, by which time they will be very hungry, and very angry. Trouble.

YOU CANNOT ALLOW YOUR CUSTOMERS TO DICTATE AT WHAT TIME THEY WILL EAT.

A restaurant must put guidelines down for the sake of its kitchen, with bookings spaced out between 7pm and 7.30pm, on to 8.30pm and 9 o'clock.

The exception to this rule is lunchtime, especially if you have a large business clientele. They have limited time, and so you solve the problem by offering a limited range of starters, one of which must be a soup (ready, warm, needs only to be ladled) and many of which should be cold. The others must be dishes which require little more than assembly, before they are whisked away to table. In the evening, a similar rule should apply, but not so rigidly.

MENU MANAGEMENT IS EVERYTHING

in terms of getting food out quickly to the customer, and speed is important when people sit down. Timing is everything. The greeting, water and bread, drinks and, then, the first food. All must flow seamlessly, for the customer is hungry, and anticipatory, and you must satisfy that appetite quickly.

Obviously the length of time can vary depending on the type of establishment, but I think a ten minute rule is a good one to set yourself. Fifteen minutes can be too long for some people, 20 minutes is generally too long for most everyone.

Customers who are eating and drinking and chatting within a quarter of an hour can then be allowed to dictate the pace somewhat, but when they come through the door, it is the restaurateur who must dictate the timing for the initial part of the evening.

SUCCESS IS A MYSTERY

What do people want?

Before we move on to some of the nuts and bolts of making a place work, let us reflect on a simple truth of the whole business of running a restaurant: Success is a mystery.

No one, but no one, can explain why certain places, people and rooms work brilliantly, and why others fail. We might remember the famous remark of the screenwriter, William Goldman, who once said that the single most important fact of Hollywood and the movie industry was that:

"Nobody knows anything".

Why draw an analogy with the movie industry? Simply because restaurants and movies have an awful lot in common. Both are entertainments where you have to persuade people through the door. Both have scripts – in the case of movies the dialogue and mise en scene, in the case of restaurants the menu and wine list – and both are trying to answer the most simple question of all: What do people want?

Nobody knows

Nobody really knows what people want. All they know is that what people want is always changing, and these days it changes every week and every month. There are no certainties in the marketplace anymore. Not only that, but there is no marketplace anymore. There are only multiple markets with multiple demands, few of which are predictable, and there is no accurate way of reading what people might want next.

Of course, people will tell you, before you open a restaurant, that you should commission market research, and use logistical analysis to find the right site, and then tie-up with a (currently) hot designer to do your interior, and if you do all of this, your restaurant will be a success.

No it won't.

When nobody knows anything, there is only one certainty by which you should be guided in the restaurant business: Fortune favours the brave.

Fortune favours the brave

Successful restaurants all come out of the blue and break the mould, and leave everyone else standing around scratching their heads asking: how did they do it? How did they know? The answer is that they didn't know, they just hoped, and they were brave. They didn't do all the sums and check all the figures and plot graphs on their PCs, because all the sums and figures and graphs and predictions and proposal plans mean nothing in the restaurant business.

The newest movie star comes out of nowhere, seemingly, but if you plot their path you will find that there has inevitably been some time spent on stage and then in minor roles, and then finally the breakthrough when the right script and the right director coincide with the emerging talent to make that breakthrough.

Restaurants operate the same way. You need to pay your dues. You need that process of education and learning, you need that time spent figuring things out and realising what you can do and what you can't do. Are you a good looking boy or girl who can handle a romantic lead but will die a thousand deaths in Shakespeare? Don't touch

Shakespeare. Are you a competent short order cook who knows how to handle a room and create a buzz but you can't hack the tall food gig and wouldn't know a celebrity from a civil servant? Open a bistro and put Burt Bacharach songs on the system.

But whilst knowing your limitations is the best guarantee that things will work, it is still not a guarantee. As William Goldman observes, regarding the movies,

"Not one person in the entire motion picture field knows for a certainty what's going to work. Every time out it's a guess – and if you're lucky, an educated one"

The educated guess

No one knows what will work and what people want, but there are certain things which will militate against running a successful restaurant. Here are the major errors people make in the business, the uneducated guesses.

The chef is God

This idea is history. People will no longer be lectured to about food, and will no longer put up with cheffy pomposity, such as refusing to put salt and pepper on the table, or refusing to cook meat anyway other than the way the chef wants to do it. Behave like this, and you are doomed.

SUCCESS IS A MYSTERY

I want to take the people somewhere new

As we have noticed, people like certainty and consistency in a restaurant. If you have been exposed to the joys of, let us say, Andean cookery on a trip through South America, and you can't wait to get back home and open the first Andean restaurant in town, you are doomed to failure. People simply won't be ready for it. If you wish to turn them on to the splendours of Andean food, do it by osmosis and attrition, slowly introducing new ideas into the context of a regular menu. You can bring an audience with you, but if you are too far ahead of them, the restaurant will not work, for they have no context in which to appraise the food, and so they will be unable to catch up with your idea, and they will go elsewhere.

It's a social thing, and I just want a beautiful room in which to entertain my friends

Bad idea. Restaurants are there for ordinary people to come and eat and enjoy themselves. If your focus is on creating someplace which is, effectively, a private dining room, the ambience will be all wrong, and the restaurant won't work. You are there to serve the customer, not to have a laugh with your friends. This is probably the cardinal sin when it comes to running a restaurant.

My wife may not be the best front of house person, but she is my wife

Oh dear. This applies to husbands as well, and we might call it the Partners Problem. He loves to cook, but she doesn't much like serving food but does it to please him (and to save wages). Disaster all round.

You cannot and should not have anyone working in a restaurant who is not committed to it. If your partner hates to work in a restaurant, then hire someone who loves the work and let your spouse find another job.

The bad vibes which emanate from a disgruntled partner poison a dining room.

I must have the hottest chef in town in my place

And, of course, the current hot shot will cost you a fortune to hire, and in six months time he will take off to another new restaurant where he will have been offered even more money, and your reputation for good food will plummet. Employing egotistical superstar chefs is a bad idea, for they have no commitment to anything other than their ego and their wallet. Get someone who loves to cook and who talks the same language as you. They will make your place a success.

The architect had a crazy idea, and we just let him go with it

And you wound up with something that has all the comfort of a fast-food joint and all the atmosphere of a deserted football stadium.

If you are employing architects and designers for your restaurant, make sure you hire people who have a feel for the job, a feel for the whole business of creating a space where people will feel comfortable, where the lighting is kind and the acoustics suitable. Don't let architects and designers railroad the design to become a private hobbyhorse. The bottom line of every restaurant is that the space must WORK.

FINDING A SIGNATURE

What is style?

The easiest way to define "style" is to say that it is so comprehensively a part of a person's personality that they are almost unaware of it.
Stylish people and stylish places are almost never self-conscious, and the fashionable belief that style makes a "statement" and that that "statement" is of necessity ephemeral is nonsense. Style is not mere fashionability. It is, instead, the discovery of a signature which relates to the way you work and expresses your beliefs and concerns.

AS IT IS WITH PEOPLE AND PLACES, SO IT IS WITH FOOD, and finding your culinary style – your culinary signature – is one of the most important things a restaurateur can achieve. Whether your fated signature is lavish – lots of flavours on the plate, lots of action with the design – or simple – let the flavours speak for themselves, and make the room as restrained as the food – what you must do is find the style, the signature, and remain true to it.

Cooking fails to work when people do something they are not truly happy with, when their style is out of step with their intent and their beliefs. The person whose fundamental nature is that of an ascetic will not like lavishness and pomp. The person who is a natural showman will not be happy in a low-profile place. Restaurants work when people do things their own way, when they bequeath their style to a room and a menu, when they let the food carry their own signature, whatever that may actually be.

A vital factor about acquiring a signature is, of course, that no one else can replicate it. They may be able to copy your decor and your menu, but they won't be able to cook like you. Finding your signature, therefore, makes each cook unique, which is how things should be.

But there is something even more fundamental to the success of a restaurant which results from the kitchen having its own signature. More than anything else, a culinary signature, a culinary style, is CONVINCING. It convinces people without you even having to try harder. A signature brings together your creativity and your ambition, and these are what persuade people to come through the door. Basically, they like what you do, they like the way you do it, and they like the fact that no one else does it that way. Think of the signature as your fingerprint: everyone is different, and can't be copied.

Coping with the critics

Food and restaurant critics have a very curious relationship with the people whose work they criticise. Restaurateurs often damn critics because they are "amateurs", i.e. not trained professionals, but who would expect a movie critic to have spent time as a best boy or third assistant director before they are allowed into print. No drama critic also needs to be a dramatist, and if they were, indeed, they would likely make very poor critics indeed.

Yet people in the restaurant business often suggest that trained professionals make good critics, and indeed some guide books use

FINDING A SIGNATURE

people who have a background in the industry as their inspectors. I don't think this is a good idea, simply because it removes the inspector or critic from the role of "ordinary customer", and I believe that that is the way in which critics should behave: just like everybody else. The critic who always eats on his own is missing out on the sociability which is one of the most important things about the restaurant experience for the vast majority of people.

Worst of all, these critics assume that criticism of restaurants can be a hierarchical process, leading to a situation where someone is "better" than someone else, and eventually leading to a situation where someone is the "best". This is simply not true.

CRITICISM SHOULD BE BASED ON THE APPRECIATION AND UNDERSTANDING not just of people's skills, but also of their ambition. Criticism should be the business of deciphering the signature of a cook and a restaurant: the critic should be looking for the writing on the food, on the walls, on the staff, on the feel of the restaurant. They should pay attention to every element of the restaurant, and know that the food is only one element, and not even the most important element when we consider what makes for a successful and enjoyable restaurant experience.

I believe that this is what critics should assess and judge and measure. Taking a hierarchical approach rules out the person who does things differently, and creates too narrow a canon of acclaim.

I think the hierarchical approach frequently leads critics astray, because they are no longer looking for the things which are truly important in restaurants and cooking – innovation, personality, signature, creativity, hospitality – but are instead reduced to a narrow canon of criticism whereby the person with the right bathrooms and drapes is, supposedly, "better" and worthy of a higher rating than the person who doesn't have the right bathrooms and drapes. It simply isn't so.

The other thing which deservedly gives critics a bad name is the fact that their judgements are often much too personal. The movie reviewer who reveres Welles and Renoir will still get a buzz out of watching "The Terminator", simply because James Cameron's movie is so well made. The critic for whom Joyce's "Ulysses" is the pinnacle of literary endeavour will still like to curl up with a zippy Elmore Leonard thriller.

But there are restaurant critics who are happy to remain ignorant of Chinese cooking, or who have never explored the variations of Italian regional cooking and whose 'critical' considerations resolve around a solipsistical and egotistical mantra: This is good, because I like it.

These people, then, have a habit of saying, "My guest didn't like her filet mignon", or "she didn't much care for her gratinated squid ink pasta with Dublin Bay prawns", as if that amounted to "criticism". It isn't criticism, merely personalised ignorance, for not only does it place a personal preference as a critical summation, it also offers no analysis as to why the dish failed, if indeed it did fail.

Critics who work like this – and often they are "celebrity" critics, folk who get the gig of reviewing restaurants because they are well known, not because they know anything about food – should be denounced by restaurateurs, because restaurateurs deserve much, much better. Running a good restaurant is one of the most difficult things anyone can set out to do, and to have some egotistical ignoramus casting unwarranted nonsense in print is simply too much to bear.

But critics no longer have the power they once had. A better educated clientele can nowadays tell when critics are out of their depth, and they will denounce anyone whose work shows no evidence of being able to analyse a meal. Nevertheless, a negative review can have an impact on a restaurant, so how do you go about combating the critics?

THE ANSWER TO A BAD REVIEW IS TO RESOLVE TO GET BETTER, and to resolve first off to build your business organically, i.e. you must appreciate that your most important critics are your customers, and not someone who writes for a newspaper or a magazine. If you have a good relationship with your customers, if you give them what they want in a space that they want to visit, then they will support you, irrespective of what anyone writes about you.

The reality is that, for everyone, there will be times when your restaurant has a bad night, and things don't go smoothly, and of course you will have critics in on that very same night. Then, you simply have to roll with the punches, painful as it may be.

On the other hand, if your restaurant is founded on a lot of hype and public relations activity, and has no organic foundation, then any adverse publicity is going to be very bad news indeed. Many new restaurants nowadays bombard critics with press releases and information, but I feel this is often counter-productive. A letter of introduction to a guide book editor, an editor or a critic, which includes your menus and wine list and some background detail, is much more effective than a glossy handout. A personal letter from a restaurateur is much more enticing than half a dozen telephone calls from a p.r. agency. The best restaurateurs communicate regularly with guide books and writers, but only by letter.

Nobody is perfect all the time, and no one expects you to be. Good critics should be able to read when things are not working, and place a review in that context, but very many are simply unable to do so.

INTERPRETING GALVIN

In the introductory pages of his collection of recipes and reminiscences, "The Drimcong Food Affair", *(MacDonald Publishing, 1992)* Gerard Galvin sketched out some of the most profound and impressive thoughts about modern restaurant practice by any working chef, in a chapter headed "Restaurant Perceptions".
Here, I would like to comment further on some of his thoughts and preoccupations.

"RESTAURATEURING IS PRIMARILY ABOUT SERVICE AND THEREFORE A WONDERFUL WAY OF LIFE"

The way in which Gerard Galvin links these two elements seems to me to be a key exposition of the success of this great chef and restaurateur. The pleasure of the work actually derives from the satisfaction given by the calling of the profession, which is the service. I think what is important about this remark is the organic nature of the relationship which it reveals.

Enjoying the service means an enjoyable profession, simple as that. If you view service as servility, you will not respect your work, as Galvin continues: "...there is a difference between service and servility. Most of us are proud of our ability to serve and actually believe it to be worthwhile. We dispense hospitality".

INTERPRETING GALVIN

"WE MUST TAKE COGNISANCE OF THE FACT THAT RESTAURANTS ARE SOMETIMES SEEN AS FEEDING POSTS FOR THE OVERFED, THE EXCLUSIVE RESORTS OF THE RICH HOSTILE TO CHILDREN, RUN BY SELF-IMPORTANT AND POMPOUS PERSONS CHARGING EXORBITANT PRICES FOR INFERIOR FOOD"

Galvin once again mercilessly exposes the question of perception, and the faults of restaurateurs who believe that a restaurant with a clientele of wealthy and famous people is somehow a "better" restaurant than one where families and people with modest means can go to enjoy themselves.

CRITICS, OF COURSE, ARE ALSO TO BLAME FOR THIS PERCEPTION, for they often confine their accolades to places where the prices are high and the furnishings sumptuous, and neglect the simple places where talented people cook with passion and care. I don't believe that anyone can truly enjoy cooking for the rich and famous. I believe that the people who run these restaurants – and there are plenty of them – are cynical and contemptible. The term "exclusive" is, in fact, anathema to the entire business of running a real restaurant.

"There is still widespread suspicion of restaurants"

I think this is declining, but it was a perception which was well founded a decade ago, and there are restaurants today who actually continue to create this suspicion. I feel the suspicion revolves mainly around the idea of value.

We can explore this quite simply: the waiter offers me a choice of breads, and I pick one or two types from the basket. What I have not noticed, because it is written at the bottom of the menu, is that there is a charge for the breads. The waiter does not explain to me that they are charged for. The breads are excellent, and the meal is good, and the final bill is high, for we have had a fine old time. But when the bill arrives, what I notice is not the total, but the amount charged for breads which I was unaware of. I pay the bill, and I resolve not to go back to the restaurant, simply because I feel I have been taken advantage of. I do not feel that the restaurant has been open and transparent with me. I believe that they have conspired to conceal a cost. I am not, of course, worried about the money, simply the issue of trust. I feel they have breached the covenant of trust which must exist in order for me to have a good time.

One small detail spoils my regard for the restaurant. I will not be back, because they have made me suspicious of their practices. Concealing details, whether it is as to cost or quality, breeds suspicion.

WE... INSTILL IN OUR STAFF THE IDEA THAT WHAT WE DO IS ENJOYABLE AND NOT WORTH DOING IF IT IS NOT.
IF WE ENJOY WHAT WE DO, THE POSITIVE ATTITUDE GETS TO THE CUSTOMER TOO"

This is one of the vital philosophical beliefs of a great restaurateur and teacher. Restaurants are an entertainment, and people go to them for enjoyment. If the staff are not getting a buzz out of the pressure and the service, the restaurant will not work. Simple as that. Positive thinking is essential for all staff, and those who find the work a chore should go and do something else.

"EATING IS MORE IMPORTANT THAN SEX — WE DO IT AT LEAST THREE TIMES A DAY AT ALL AGES AND YET IT MERITS LITTLE PLANNING AND INSUFFICIENT TIME BOTH IN THE PREPARATION AND THE PARTAKING. IT IS A SOURCE OF PLEASURE BEYOND COMPARE"

Each and every one of us will have to decide if we agree with Gerard Galvin as to the relative importance of sex and eating! But what is crucial here is the acknowledgment that eating "is a source of pleasure beyond compare". No one can disagree with that, and even though Galvin is alluding to the domestic kitchen when he says that we devote insufficient time to the preparation and partaking of food, it is a point which every chef should remember when it comes to their own domestic cooking, and indeed to cooking the staff dinner: there should be no such thing as "staff food", for the staff should eat the menu that is being served, and know it and appreciate it as well as anyone.

"I HAVE NO DOUBT THAT THE APPRECIATION OF FOOD AND WINE HAS A CIVILISING INFLUENCE. THERE IS A DIRECT RELATIONSHIP BETWEEN CARE FOR WHAT WE EAT AND DRINK AND OUR ATTITUDE TO LAND, LIVESTOCK AND ENVIRONMENT. PUT SIMPLY, IF YOU VALUE THE PURITY AND RICHNESS OF A FREE RANGE EGG, YOU ARE LESS LIKELY TO APPROVE OF MASS PRODUCTION AND INTENSIVE FARMING"

How interesting that Galvin should reduce this important question down to the chicken and the egg, but it is apt, for the hideous treatment in which battery hens are reared means that their eggs are hardly with eating.

Every chef and restaurateur has a duty to their customers to source the very best materials they can, and if they have any reservations about the production methods of food, then they should not put it on the menu. We will not be able to improve food production standards unless people in high-profile positions assert that their responsibility extends to knowing the source and treatment of their raw ingredients.

The flip side of this, of course, is that food which is reared humanely is superior in taste and texture to mass produced food. If you want to be known as a great cook, you won't be able to do it unless you have the best ingredients. But what is also significant about this statement is the relationships it suggests: the civilising influence of food and wine should make us respect our relationship with food production and the environment.

All are connected. Food does not simply arrive on a plate, and those who close their eyes to hideous production methods are irresponsible.

"ONE OF THE MAIN PROBLEMS THAT PEOPLE FACE IN OUR TRADE IS THAT THEY DO BECOME BOGGED DOWN IN THEIR OWN AFFAIRS AND MISS OUT ON A WIDER APPRECIATION OF LIFE. THERE IS MORE TO LIFE THAN THE WONDERS OF THE TABLE"

Indeed there is, and having a wider appreciation of the other artistic callings of life is, I would suggest, essential for the continuing development of every chef. Cooks and restaurateurs should see their roles as being capable of continuing, gradual change, and as they mature, so should their restaurants. They need, therefore, to read and to travel, to explore new fashions and ideas in food, they need to eat in the restaurants of their peers and to learn from them. They need, in a word, to be open: to new ideas, experiences, influences.

WRITING A MENU

There is something splendidly nostalgic in the act of looking back at age-old menus from the grand restaurants and hotels of yesteryear. Bulky, detailed, written largely in French, they seem to belong not just to another age, but to another planet altogether.

The menu from Luchow's, reprinted in Ludwig Bemelman's book "La Bonne Table", features 22 varieties and variations of salad, 22 daily specials, 16 versions of steak and chops, 14 varieties of ice cream dishes, alongside appetisers, oysters and clams, cold dishes, fish and seafood, specials to order, house specialities, cheese dishes, rarebits, pastries, fruits and compotes, coffees and teas.

The menu from the Lucas-Carton featured in the book is smaller, but still gargantuan, as is that of Laperouse and Le Pavillon. Basically, they offered everything except the kitchen sink.

Those days have vanished completely. Fashionable restaurants today have menus which are often starkly simple, for the new signature of authenticity is to offer less, and thereby assure the customer that they are getting more, i.e. they are getting food which is seasonal and of top quality, and nothing which does not fit those criteria makes it onto the menu.

WRITING A MENU

THE STYLE WHICH HAS RETURNED TO MENU WRITING IS SIMPLICITY. The menu at the fashionable Tribeca, in New York, offers dishes such as: fried oysters with Thai marinated vegetables; sautéed salmon with lemon and herbs; roast chicken with whipped potatoes, root vegetables; chocolate torte.

Alice Waters' menus at Chez Panisse, the inimitable institution she created at Berkeley in California, will offer dishes such as: baked goat's cheese with Heidi's garden lettuce; cured Wildwood pork roast with artichoke and potato gratin, stewed chard and shallot confit; baked California salmon with sugar snap peas, leeks, squash, potatoes and beet relish; blood orange sherbet with strawberries. The downstairs dinner menu might be as simple as this: warm asparagus salad with morels, Parmesan and pancetta; spit-roasted young chicken rubbed with garlic and thyme, balsamic vinegar sauce and fava bean risotto; apple galette with warm sabayon.

In Wolfgang Puck's legendary restaurant, Spago, menus offer dishes such as: tempura lemon sole with three colour tomatoes and basil vinaigrette; pizza with spicy chicken, roasted peppers and sweet onions; grilled free range chicken with double blanched garlic and Italian parsley.

LET US LOOK AT TWO IRISH EXAMPLES.

Here are some dishes from Eugene Callaghan's menu at La Marine Bistro, in Rosslare: grilled Bannow Bay mussels with a garlic and pinenut crumb; pasta quills with sautéed Kilmore Quay scallops, crispy bacon and garlic; roast rack of Rosslare lamb with gratin of Mediterranean vegetables and pasta; Eugene's baked cheesecake with ice cream and summer fruit compote.

And here are some dishes from Longueville House, in County Cork, where William O'Callaghan is the chef: terrine of Longueville pork pâté with a garden plum chutney and salad; slices of house smoked Blackwater River salmon with a garden salad, gribiche sauce; loin of

Longueville lamb baked in a potato and herb crust, tarragon sauce; roast loin of venison with parsnip pancake and wild rice, it's juices flavoured with Chinese pepper; flat garden apple tart with Calvados ice cream and caramel sauce.

Let us draw down some rules from these transatlantic examples.

No language other than a concise summation of the contents of the dish is permitted

FLOWERY, DESCRIPTIVE LANGUAGE IS DISASTROUS ON A MENU. It reads badly, and looks even worse. Food does not "rest on a bed of" vegetables. Beds are what we sleep in, we don't put them onto plates. You do not "coat", "drape" and "top" with sauces: you do not use French terms which people do not understand. This applies to titles as well, so desserts are not "endings". The chosen menus tell us all we need to know in language which is accurate and informative. There are no adjectives, traditionally the most annoying aspect of badly written menus. If the lamb you are cooking is tender, then you never say it: you let the customer find out for themselves. Salads should never be described as "freshly gathered", as we are entitled to presume that they are just so, and we wouldn't order them if they weren't. Less is more when writing a menu.

The language is precise

You cannot write menus with alleged dishes such as: Chef's Vegetarian Choice. What on earth is that, and what on earth is in it? We don't know, and by not knowing we are dissuaded from trying it. You must tell people what is going to be on the plate. Soup du Jour and Pâté Maison are two other dinosaur terms which put people off. If the pâté is made with chicken livers, then it is Chicken Liver Pâté.

WRITING A MENU

Never conceal or obfuscate, let people know what is involved in the dish.

The language specifies the origin of the food

Look at how the food in Chez Panisse, La Marine and Longueville House carries its sources: Heidi's salad; Wildwood pork; Bannow Bay mussels; Longueville pork; garden apple tart. This is very wise, and very appealing. If something comes from a particular area which is renowned for good produce, then let people know just what you have. If it comes from a particular grower, or, even better, is grown and produced by you, then that is very important indeed. This identification of origin is one of the most reassuring things you can write on a menu, and whilst it is obviously more difficult to achieve in a large city restaurant, it should still be done whenever you can, even if it is to simply specify the port where your fish was landed.

The language specifies the seasonality of the food

Gerard Galvin has written that menus should be "short, seasonal, and understandable". Obviously, menus in places such as bistros are inclined to be less seasonal than in restaurants, but seasonality is vital, and should be an element of every menu, even if the only way you can introduce it is via daily dishes chalked on a blackboard. You should not offer salmon all year round, for example, because the salmon season is restricted. But when fish, vegetables and fruits are in season, or when you have new season lamb, this must be trumpeted on the menu, for it reveals that not only are you serious, but that you appreciate and understand the food chain.

The language tells you only what you need to know

This is a key factor. If you describe a dish down to the last detail, then there will be no element of surprise for the customer when the dish arrives. If a dish of "Sea bass, new potatoes, tomato and tarragon sauce" features a clever display of rod-caught fish and an intricate sauce with the freshest garden tarragon and ripe, local tomatoes, then both the presentation and the flavourfulness of the food will give the customer unexpected pleasure. Never overstate your case in writing, do it on the plate, for that is how you will win over the customer. If you overstate the case on the menu, and the dish arrives and falls short of the customer's expectations, then you have a problem, for they are immediately disappointed, and you will not be able to win them back again. Make sure the magic is on the plate, and not in the prose.

Handwritten is best

A handwritten menu is the most delightful thing in the world, but few restaurants have the time to do it, and most use a database from which they draw upon dishes. If you can't write by hand, at least try to put the date on the menu. In the performance of the dinner, customers want to know that tonight's performance has been worked on today.

No menu is a good thing

It might sound like the restaurateur's nightmare, but very many people enjoy not being handed a menu. If you have the confidence, and the right clientele, and the right sort of establishment, then you can get away with not writing a menu, but simply cooking what has arrived that day. A minority proposition, perhaps, but not as scary or as alienating as restaurateurs often think it is. Many people enjoy the surprise menu which restaurateurs like William O'Callaghan of Longueville House, in County Cork, offer each night.

A menu must be balanced

It must offer meat, fish, and vegetarian choices, it should always offer a salad and cheeses, and the starters should echo the main courses in terms of variety, colour and composition, and all this must be done without seeming to try too hard. A dinner menu from The Mermaid Café, in Dublin's Temple Bar, offers seven starters, eight main courses, five desserts and cheese. The starters include: aubergine, red pepper and goats cheese terrine with oregano and pepper sauce; mussel chowder with celery biscuits; smoked eel and new season potato salad with horseradish and sour cream, as well as a lettuce and artichoke salad and a dish of antipasti. The main courses have char-grilled rib eye steak; asparagus, pecorino and poached egg calzone; artichoke and cannellini bean compote; pork and black pudding with cumin spiced beetroot. There is argentin cake and pecan pie for dessert, with summer pudding, today's ice cream with home-made tuile, and the Irish cheeses come with apricot chutney and celery biscuits.

THAT IS HOW YOU DO IT. New season potato salad. A clever folded pizza. Lots of choices for vegetarians. Today's ice cream. Summer pudding. Irish cheeses. Balance, specificity, interest, variety, food which customers want to eat and which is also – and this is vital – food which is interesting for the kitchen to cook.

The price

Customers should know exactly how much a meal will cost them. If you have a fixed price dinner, then there should be nothing added to it in any shape or form, and the fixed price should include whatever service charge you include.

THE MISTAKES WHICH RESTAURATEURS MAKE REGARDING PRICING ARE:

● Charging for breads, and the cardinal sin of charging for breads and not making it clear that there is a charge.
This is one of the most irritating things for restaurant customers.

● Having a fixed price menu, but then building too many supplements into it for various dishes.
Again, this is simply annoying. If there is a supplement for the starter you want and the main course, then where is the "fixed price"?

● Charging a service charge and not making it clear that tipping is not expected.
Indeed, many restaurants compound this mistake by also leaving a space at the bottom of the credit card slip for a gratuity. This is foolish. If people want to tip on top of a service charge, they will do so. To expect them to tip and pay service is bad manners.

● Adding a blanket service charge which includes drinks and wines. A major cause of annoyance for customers, particularly if a large group has a lot of wine to drink and are paying service for each and every bottle.

In an ideal restaurant, there should only be a service charge for groups of 6 or more. If there is a service charge, then it should be specified on the menu that it is distributed evenly amongst the floor staff. Service charge should not be levied on drinks and wine. This way is transparent and open, people know exactly how much they will pay, and they will trust you.

WRITING A WINE LIST

If menus are frequently the most self-indulgent area to be found in a restaurant, then they are super-seded only by the utter pomposity and selfishness which is evident in dozens of wine lists.

We all know the type: pages and pages of print packed with useless, meaningless language, which tells us nothing about the bottles for sale and everything about this private hobby-horse of the owner. Added to this useless verbosity will be the further insult that the owner once had a holiday in the Barossa Valley, and is determined that we should know it. So, an entire page will be sacrificed to a selection of wines from that region, which completely overbalances the list and simply makes it look foolish.

A good wine list is like a good wine

All good wines are similar. They have style, they have varietal character, they speak of the region from which they come, and they reflect the care and passion of the winemaker. Every good wine list should do exactly the same thing.

The style comes from the language used, and the precision with which it is used. The wine list from Belfast restaurateur Nick Price's Warehouse describes La Chablisienne Chablis AC as: "Butter and lemon and superb value from the leading Co-op in Chablis. We highly recommend it".

In two short sentences we know the basic style of the wine, we appreciate that whilst other wines from this area cost a lot we have stumbled upon a bottle at the right price, and we know something of the status and method of production of the wine: it is not made by a single grower, but by a respected Co-op. Finally, it is given the restaurateur's recommendation.

To give us all of that information in simple language in a pair of sentences is remarkable, and effective, and the net result is simple: we will order the wine.

IMAGINE IF THE DESCRIPTION HAD READ:

"Chablis is a region in the north of France where the permitted grape varieties are, as elsewhere, restricted, and it is generally dealt with in texts as part of Burgundy, despite lying further north than Burgundy proper. There are seven grand cru designations and an increasing number of premier cru sites. Ainsworth describes the wines as "apple-crisp, greeny-gold, bone-dry, in some years slightly tart", whilst Parker marks out two fundamental Chablis styles, those fermented and aged in stainless steel, and those which are barrel-fermented and oak-aged".

The important thing about this imaginary text is that none of it is incorrect, but it is completely useless. Who are Ainsworth and Parker, asks the layman? If grape varieties are restricted, what are they restricted to? If there are two distinct styles of Burgundy, then what style is the wine we are being offered? Why tell us about grand cru and premier cru sites if the wine on the list is a straightforward Chablis?

A LITTLE KNOWLEDGE, AS THIS DEMONSTRATES, IS A DANGEROUS THING

when it comes to writing a wine list. The correct way to use knowledge when writing a wine list is to write exactly what your customers require. If you run a simple place where people will not be used to drinking wine regularly, then the language should be devoid of any "wine-speak", i.e. the "*cigar box aromas, excellent length and a smoother finish than the celebrated '92 vintage"* which so many writers fall captive to.

Here is the kind of thing I mean. This is part of a list I wrote which was designed to entice people to choose a bottle, even if those people have yet to learn about the basic grape varieties.

THE WINE LIST

Our wine list has been chosen to offer wines which we believe are great fun and great value. If we can be of any assistance in helping you to choose a wine, then please ask.

BRILLIANT BARGAINS: WINES UNDER £10

White Wines

CHILE: SANTIAGO CHARDONNAY–SEMILLON 1996

This blend of everyone's favourite white wine grapes, chardonnay and semillon, makes for a deliciously refreshing wine, choc-a-bloc with light, spicy flavours and just perfect for zingy chicken dishes and full-flavoured pastas.

CHILE: SANTIAGO SAUVIGNON BLANC 1997

A lovely, lemony, smoky white wine, gloriously refreshing, and with a crisp kiss of fresh fruit flavours like apricots, peaches and limes in every sip.

AUSTRALIA: CANOE TREE DRY WHITE 1996

Canoe Tree is a punchy white wine with unrestrained, thirst-quenching freshness and oodles of fruit flavours all ready to kick in with every sip. Fab winemaking.

Red Wines

Red Wines

CHILE: SANTIAGO CABERNET SAUVIGNON 1996

Packed with jammy, strawberry scents and comforting, warming plummy flavours, this red wine is medium bodied and delicately spicy, and your steak needs a bottle of this right now.

AUSTRALIA CANOE TREE DRY RED 1996
A terrific, light, Aussie red wine with lots of lovely, friendly fruit flavours
and scents of toffee and sweet sticky things like bananas. Delightful.

ITALY: MONTEPULCIANO D'ABRUZZO 1996
Never mind what the name means, just try this voluptuous, graceful glass
of red wine and see what modern Italian winemaking is all about. Slightly
dry and very easy to drink, this is gorgeous. The full Monte!

FRANCE: DOMAINE DES SALICES MERLOT 1995
This is so slinky and sublime it's the wine equivalent of an Yves St. Laurent
little black number. A truly, typically French red wine which uses the merlot
grape to produce a very full yet quite dry flavour, this is very moreish, very
fashionable.

THIS WAS THE INTRODUCTORY SECTION OF THE LIST,
which was also unusual in being sourced from one supplier, done for
simplicity's sake. There is no "wine-speak", and comparisons
regarding the wines are drawn from the mainstream culture – movies,
fashion, and so on. The language is deliberately flippant and jokey, in
order to make the list more approachable, and it invites the customer
to ask the staff for help.
The bottom line, I suppose, is that the list proved to be a practical
success; wine sales increased substantially, and people who came to
the hotel/restaurant who had never ordered a bottle of wine before
began to do so.

Medium body, good length, great legs, smooth finish

If you have an audience who are already familiar with wine, then you
need to do two things. The first is to write your list crisply and clearly
and without cliché. If you tumble into the "medium bodied, smooth

WRITING A WINE LIST

finish and good length with a touch of leather", then your hip audience will know that you don't know what language you need to describe the wine.

The second consideration is sourcing the wines themselves. You cannot source from a single supplier if you want a serious list, and you certainly cannot let the supplier write your list for you, as used to be the case with so many Chinese restaurants in the past. People who have drank countless bottles of different wines will be bored by a list they are already familiar with, whereas if you offer them something unexpected, and you describe it well, then you entice them immediately, and this is what a good list is all about: enticement.

Here is the sort of thing I mean. The wine list in The Mermaid Café, in Dublin's Temple Bar, announces "All our wines are imported directly by The Mermaid Café", and offers a variety of aperitifs, a good selection of soft drinks, then a pair of red and white house wines and a page of white wines and a page of red wines.

Amongst the red wines, number 44 is described thus: "Pellegrini Carignane 1994 (California). California's little secret comes to light. Beloved of Cal/Ital wine growers, this varietal is crammed with ripe cherry fruit, delicate spices and a little oaky earthiness. Well known in Southern France as the backbone of hearty wines".

Number 45 is described thus: "Faugeres Rouge Valinere 1993 (Faugeres). A really special wine. 100% Mourvedre. With the rediscovery of the virtues of old varietals made with modern techniques, Mourvedre is an important source of rich, complex wines, often suffused with aromas of blackberry fruit, warm herbs and the exotic suggestion of Southern pine woods".

THIS IS IMPRESSIVE, LEARNED AND USEFUL WINE WRITING. It lets us know the quirks and history of what the bottles offer, along with concise notes about style which avoid any "wine-speak". It is also enthusiastic, and remember that the wine list is an important part of that propositional element which you need to offer when people come into the restaurant. It makes you want to try these wines, makes you want to explore beyond chardonnay and cabernet sauvignon.

Here is another way to do it right, from The Green Onion Caffé, in Limerick, a funky, fun place with hip staff.

"Chapelle d'Auriol, Corbiere Rouge, France, 1995. This is a gushy, fruity, juicy wine from the local grenache, syrah and carignane grapes. Black as the ace of spades, more supple than a drunken limbo dancer. Well worth checking out".

"Alamos Ridge Cabernet Sauvignon, Argentina, 1993. This is a warm and loving cabernet sauvignon with oodles of comforting autumn berry fruits gently girded with a firm enough corsetry of ripe tannins and acids to soothe the soul. Life affirming".

This is excellent, fun writing, which perfectly matches the mood of the place, and which uses the same language to describe its wines as the customers would use to describe their latest c.d. Concise, enthusiastic, it presumes no knowledge on the part of the customer, and offers them an introduction and an enticement. Best of all, the list lets you know exactly what to expect, which is the key to good wine writing.

IF YOU ARE ENTHUSIASTIC ABOUT WINE, the greatest thing you can do is to encourage your staff to get interested in it also. If you do this, they will sell the wine for you, because they will know exactly what they are talking about, and they will themselves recommend wines to customers, simply by gleaning what the customer likes and what they are going to order.

If you have a specialist sommelier, then that is fortunate, but not necessary. Everyone enjoys wine and is intrigued by it, and if you turn your staff on to the pleasures of the game, then you will find the wines will sell better than ever, and the relationship between staff and customers will improve greatly. Everyone loves to recommend a wine which the customer is happy with. So, tastings with the staff are essential, an essential part of their education, which we shall explore next.

TRAINING STAFF

Disharmony breeds discontent

A creative, consistent kitchen produces creative, consistent food, and is staffed with creative, calm people who achieve above and beyond what they should ordinarily be capable of. This is the ideal to aim for when it comes to selecting and training staff. Restaurants are creative places, and no one – but no one – produces their best in an atmosphere of conflict and turmoil.

This should be so obvious as to be uncontestable, but strangely enough, there are cooks who reckon that you need a macho, state-of-emergency atmosphere to prevail in a kitchen. And so, they create that atmosphere, by means of intimidatory behaviour and verbal – and even physical – abuse. These people are foolish megalomaniacs, and anyone who finds themselves in a kitchen or a restaurant where this currency is common should get out the door as quick as possible.

A little bit of calm

In the appendix to this book which deals with a day in the life of Roly's Bistro, I witnessed one moment of panic during the seventeen or eighteen hours I was there. This was when stock-taking revealed a shortfall of some steaks, and there was a brief panic until they were found. Otherwise, that sleek machine pulsed effectively and efficiently for an entire day when five hundred or so people were fed and had a high old time. That is what restaurants should all be like. Everyone knew what they had to do, and they simply did it, and thereby enjoyed it.

The main benefits from this sort of inspired delegation are the integrity and confidence which it gives to the cooks, and the characterful confidence it gives to the staff. We all know the situation where floor staff are not relaxed, and what usually causes this is bad management. But, if you select the right people to work and then let them get on with it, their confidence blooms as they come into contact with people. This is vitally important, for the way in which food is served to table is integral to the nature, style and success of a restaurant. So, the ideal way to train staff is as follows:

Select the right person

You have to be able to spot them a mile away, and be able to spot the sort of characteristics which tell you that someone will be efficient, motivated and pleasurable to work with. And, you have to bear in mind that there are many people who simply do not have what it takes. They are not good at engaging people, or else they are not an efficient, harmonious presence in the kitchen.

Basically, the person who starts off by asking: what do I get paid, and how much time off do I get? is not the sort of person you want in your restaurant. This is a creative business, and you need to find the people who are basically looking for a job which allows them to express themselves. For many restaurateurs, that person today is often a thirtysomething who walks in the door and says: "I hate banking, and I love to cook. Can I have a job?". If they walk in your door, you say yes, straightaway.

DON'T HIRE SOMEONE JUST BECAUSE THEY HAVE PASSED ALL THEIR EXAMS and have every certificate under the sun. You still need to suss out whether or not they are creative and can handle the pressure, or are they better suited to the classroom atmosphere in which they have done so well? Having a brace of exam passes and degrees by itself means nothing.

Show them how to do what you want them to do

Part of the style of any restaurant is the face which the staff put on for the customers. If you run a joint where the waitresses have to slam tequilas and stand on tables and sing, then you have to show them the best and most charming ways in which to do those ridiculous things. The point is: don't expect people to be able to cope without having your style explained and demonstrated to them. If you have a formal restaurant, then you will have to explain to them how to stand still and keep their hands behind their back. Whatever the style, they must be shown what is expected.

THE SAME IS TRUE OF THE KITCHEN. New cooks must be inducted into the style of the restaurant's food, but what you should try to discover here, after they have learnt the ropes, is if they have anything to contribute to the cooking style, or any new spins and improvisations which will make your food even better. If you get the best out of them, they are simultaneously getting the best out of themselves, and they are happy cooks, happy staff, people relishing the buzz and the pressure.

Handling the pressure

The time factor involved in cooking means that one must cope with constant pressure. Many people simply cannot hack this, and they should be directed towards another career as fast as you can get them out the door. The old cliché is a constant: if you can't stand the heat, get out of the kitchen.

Training the locals

Some restaurants believe that attracting a high-profile chef and pandering to (inevitably his) ego is how you run a restaurant. This is a disastrous idea. Egomaniacs are the very worst chefs, often unwilling to share any secrets with their team, people who believe the job exists for their greater glory, and who always have an eye out for the next opportunity, when they will walk out the door straight away. Never hire celebrity chefs. Work with local people, who will be honoured to be given the job, and train them to do things properly, and unleash their creativity. The happiest kitchens are staffed by local men and women who are enjoying the pressure, working together, laughing together, and sending out knock-out food. No chef is an island; they must be team players, or else they should not be in a kitchen. If everyone in a restaurant does not pull together, constantly reading one another's minds as the madness of service develops all around them, constantly covering for others and making sure that the performance goes as smoothly as possible, then the dream of consistent, creative food in a charming atmosphere will not happen.

Scrap the staff dinner

The staff in a restaurant should eat the food they cook for the customers, not simply because they are every bit as good as the customers and every bit as deserving, but also because they need to understand, as a community of people, exactly what the food is all about and what the restaurant is trying to achieve with the food. The same is true of the wine list: they should understand it and be familiar with it, but not too familiar, of course.

There are no rules

As with so many other situations in the restaurant business, there are no hard and fast rules when it comes to staff. The timid little chef may turn into the greatest patissier ever born. The shy little girl may become the greatest floor manager the city has ever seen. The secret of working with people in a restaurant environment is to try to find ways in which to allow them to be creative, and to contribute in a meaningful way to the success of the restaurant.

A HAPPY ATMOSPHERE BREEDS HAPPY STAFF,

and happy staff give their best when they are appreciated. There should be bonus schemes in operation, and a sense of sharing in the rewards when the restaurant hits good times and makes money.

The staff must be involved in the entire project and vision of the restaurant. Otherwise, they will never be more than part-timers who work by rote and can't wait to knock off work. Treat them right, and they in turn will treat the customers right, and suddenly everyone is having a great time and enjoying it, and feeding off the magical energy of the restaurant entertainment.

SOURCING SUPPLIES

What is Quality?

A bloke turns up at the kitchen door. "Look", he says, "but I just came across this stash of Rolex watches, met a guy in a pub, pristine they are, and I know I'm a fool to myself, but I'm letting them go at half nothing. They're real, swear to God, and all I'm looking for is fifty sheets each". What do you do? Send him packing, of course. He's a fraud, the watches are a fraud, the story is a fraud, everything is well dodgy.

A bloke turns up at the kitchen door. "Look", he says, "but I'm just doing a friend a favour, and I swear this is the best Tipperary beef you can find, it's from his own farm. Interested? I'll do you the best price". What do you do? You should send him packing, of course. He's a fraud, the beef is a fraud, the story is a fraud, everything is well dodgy. But some people don't. Some people are suckered by the idea of a bargain, and some people believe that the idea of "quality" ingredients – i.e. ingredients which are produced to the highest possible standards and which are traceable right back to source – isn't something which needs to concern them in the running of a restaurant. They see only margins, bottom lines – "If I save X pounds and shift this quickly, then I'm quids in".

SOURCING SUPPLIES

THE IDEA OF SAVING MONEY BY COMPROMISING ON QUALITY – and by fixing private arrangements with suppliers – is one of the sicknesses of the restaurant trade. The only bottom line which should concern any restaurateur at that point when supplies are coming in the kitchen door is this: no cook, no matter how talented, can produce exciting, vivid food from undistinguished, compromised ingredients, whereas if you start from the position of using decent ingredients, then you have a better than average chance of producing creative, enjoyable food.

Quality must be everywhere

True quality begins with sourcing the very best ingredients. Quality implies a true relationship with a supplier, and by a supplier I do not mean a wholesaler, who deals in the particular commodity, i.e. fruit and vegetables, meat, eggs, bread, you name it. The restaurateur who is truly committed, who is genuinely seeking and searching for the very best, should know the provenance and background of all that he cooks and sells. He must control the food chain which, in effect, culminates at his restaurant. The great chefs all do this. They appreciate and understand how ingredients change throughout the year because they know them so intimately.

THE KEY PEOPLE YOU NEED, THEN, ARE: The best Butcher, The best Fishmonger, A supplier of Game, The best Organic Vegetable grower, The best Fruit Grower, Local Speciality Suppliers: cheese, smoked foods, chocolate, coffee.

The best butcher

The best butcher is usually easy to find in any location, and what we are looking for here is a butcher who, preferably, has his own farm, or at least has his own abattoir. If you can't find someone with these characteristics – and the idea of finding someone who has a small abattoir in certain parts of the country is remote – then you are taking a risk with the consistency and quality of the meat you will be selling.

The other test of the butcher should be his willingness to prepare unusual cuts for you – many years ago, we first heard about the arrival back in Ireland of one of the country's leading chefs when a butcher told us: "You should check this fella out. He's asking for all sorts of weird stuff!" So, make sure you ask them for the weird stuff. The benefit of this sort of care, of course, is also the question of trust at a time when many people are suspicious of meat, and there is also the benefit of being able to describe the provenance of your meat on the menu: "O'Driscoll's organically reared Tipperary fillet" sure sounds a lot more interesting than "Pan fried fillet of beef". Of course, the final benefit is that meat with intrinsic quality needs little to be done to it: the flavour is all there for you, and all you have to do is cook it to unleash it.

The best fishmonger

With fish, freshness is everything.
Once a piece of fish has gone past its best, then there is nothing, but nothing, you can do to retrieve the natural flavours.

BUT FINDING A GOOD FISHMONGER IS DIFFICULT, indeed it is one of the most difficult tasks facing any restaurateur. There has been a steady decline in the number of fishmongers in the country in recent years, trawlers have increased in size and increased the amount of time they spend at sea, and the price of fish has rocketed, yet curiously more and more people are ordering fish in restaurants these days, largely because they are timid about cooking it at home.

So, a good fishmonger is vital, indispensable, and if you find one, then look after him well, and be prepared to pay the top price for the best fish. There is no better way to carve out a fine reputation, incidentally, then being able to offer great fish and shellfish dishes, and some of the most celebrated restaurants are celebrated precisely because of their skill with fish cookery. Good fish cookery also allows you more room to offer variety on a menu, and gives more room for experimentation in the kitchen.

The game man

I suspect game will steadily make more impression on restaurant menus in years to come, and every good restaurateur should try to find a source of wild game. It is something which few domestic cooks bother with these days, so there is an added fillip in the fact that it offers new tastes, and of course is intensely seasonal.

Its wild nature also means that it is unmediated and trustworthy. In a restaurant in France, many years ago, I saw a man bring a brace of game straight through the dining room and into the kitchen. I thought it impressive, rather effective, and daring, but I appreciate that it is perhaps not to everyone's taste.

The best vegetable grower

This is perhaps the most important supplier of them all. The flavour and variety of so many vegetables has been traduced so much in recent years that they are scarcely worth cooking. So, to operate at your very best, you need vegetables which are distinctive, flavourful, and, preferably, apposite and unusual.

In Assolas Country House, for example, Hazel Bourke only makes her gloriously simple salad of mussels and potatoes when her garden crop of Catriona potatoes are ready to be harvested. They are the best variety for the dish, the most suitable and appropriate, and so the dish waits until they are ready.

The arrival of vegetables at their very best can cause great excitement and creativity in a kitchen, and I would suggest that this is the ideal way for a kitchen to operate. You must seize the seasons, and cook the food at its best time. Offering a dish on the menu all year round, irrespective of its seasonality, is ridiculous, and wholly inappropriate to a good restaurant. Vegetables which are past their best and over-mature excite no one.

If you want the weird stuff from your butcher, what you want from your vegetable grower is all sorts of "queer gear". Good growers love producing more exotic varieties of vegetables and herbs, and these are the sorts of details which will give you an edge. Remember, at this point, the aphorism of Nicholas Freeling, who wrote:

"Don't go to a restaurant for something you can do better at home"

You will not attract the interested eaters who are also the most appreciative restaurant customers, unless your menus are offering surprise and challenge. To offer this, you need a close relationship with your grower, you need to have him produce unusual foods for you.

Organic food production

And this brings us to a key point in modern food production. If you can, you should always source organically produced food, and state that you do so on the menu. I am not suggesting this for any polemical reason, though I could offer many. I will confine my advocacy to a simple, undeniable fact: organically produced food tastes better. It tastes truer, more balanced and natural, it has better cooking characteristics and texture. It is, quite simply, superior.

The best fruit grower

Commercially produced fruit, like much intensively farmed food, is largely uninteresting, so one needs to look beyond the people who

77

SOURCING SUPPLIES

simply bring all the fruit and vegetables on a truck and can offer nothing more than the most obvious – and tasteless – varieties, and offer them all year round.

Fruit, like vegetables, meat, cheeses and all the other supplies of a good restaurant, needs to be tasted and tasted and tasted. It needs to be at its best and its ripest when served, and I look forward to the day when fruit is so well sourced and understood that a simple fruit plate is offered at the end of a meal, as is the tradition in mainland European countries where diversity and suitability are appreciated.

Local Speciality Suppliers:
The cheesemonger

EVERYONE NEEDS A GOOD CHEESEMONGER, for the simple reason that if you want to serve a cheeseboard with various cheeses at their very best, to do so is a task beyond almost every restaurant. You need a specialist affineur, who knows and understands all the cheeses, knows how long they require to mature, and knows just when they are ready. The true affineur also has the correct facilities for ripening cheese, which restaurants will not have. The cheesemonger, in other words, is the person who will do the work for you, so let him do it, and deliver it when the cheeses are ready. Don't serve cheeses when they are not ripe, and above all make sure the staff know just what cheeses are on the board. Getting the names and styles of cheeses wrong is one of the most common mistakes made by waiters, and one of the least excusable.

One other rule should always be observed with cheese: make sure, if there is a local cheese, that it is always on your cheeseboard.

Smoked foods

Wild smoked salmon is one of the speciality foods most closely associated with Ireland, and it is also one of the best loved foods. And, like so many other noble foods, its quality has been traduced by poor quality farmed fish flooding the market.

There are truly expert fish smokers at work, and those are the people who restaurateurs should be seeking out. Again, the rule is to taste and taste again. The difference in quality between fine fish and farmed fish is obvious, but with tasting you will also realise that the skill of the fish smoker is of vital importance.

All smoked fish – or smoked chicken or whatever – is not the same, and you should look for the producer who is the most gifted and committed. Remember, also, that the foods are available by mail order: distance is no object.

Chocolate

Once again, there is a small amount of fine chocolate produced in the world, and a lot of rubbish which should not be allowed to call itself chocolate. Learn the difference, and only use the good stuff.

The detail of chocolate is one of the key elements which makes a great patissier.

Coffee

The quality of a restaurant's coffee is one of the most vital elements. As it ends the meal, the coffee is perhaps the final flavour which the customer enjoys, and so it must be right. As well as using good coffee, you must also know the techniques and skills involved in making perfect espressos and cappuccinos, and you must know that the technique involved in making these drinks is considerable, and is not something you do just by pushing buttons.

The same is, of course, true of tea. Irish teas are of superb quality, but many restaurants have a lot to learn as regards infusions, herbal teas and tisanes.

THE DETAILS

Waiter, there's a fly in my soup: Handling Complaints

COMPLAINTS DIVIDE, APPROXIMATELY, INTO TWO TYPES.

There are those which are genuine, which is to say that the cook has overlooked a slug happily embedded in a lettuce leaf, and leaf and slug makes its way out to the customer.

Then, there are those complaints where a customer orders a dish, and then finds, when it arrives, that it is not what they expected, or, as they will tell you, "the dish is not right".

Both types of complaint, the first where the customer is right, the second where the customer is wrong, should be treated identically. Whisk away the plate, apologise (no matter how difficult that may be), and offer them something else. If they don't want something else, don't charge them for the plate. If you want to copperfasten things, offer them a glass of wine on the house.

The reason for treating complaints in an identical fashion is not so that you can work on your heroic forbearance, but because you don't want the bleating of an ignorant customer to upset the equilibrium of the room. Confine and control the complaint as quickly as you can. As a critic, a substantial minority of letters I receive from readers relate not to how a cause for complaint arose, but how it was dealt with. A complaint dealt with efficiently and quickly has the sting drawn from it. A complaint allowed to fester will upset an entire table, who will quickly spread their poison all around the room. You cannot afford to let this happen.

THE RULE, I SUPPOSE, IS THAT, YES, THE CUSTOMER IS ALWAYS RIGHT, even when the customer is wrong. But if you wish to challenge a customer who is in the wrong, you simply make matters much, much worse. Ignorant customers are to be pitied, not humiliated. You will always have ignorant customers, most especially men who wish to showoff in front of their colleagues and families. Don't allow them to knock you off your stride.

OF COURSE, IF YOU DEAL PROPERLY WITH THE GENUINE COMPLAINT, then you will likely create a customer for life.

Setting a Table

Happily, there is no longer a fixed code as to what constitutes a properly laid table, and nor should there be. A battery of knives and forks intimidates the living daylights out of everyone these days, and simplicity is, for everyone's sake, much to be preferred.
The only question which one needs to decide, then, is just how simple you should keep things. Should the knife and fork simply rest on a napkin on a side plate? Should you take time – waste time – folding napkins into elaborate cornettos and the like? Indeed, one of the

crucial questions any restaurateur must answer is the question of napkins and tablecloths: paper or cloth? Starched or not?

The answer, here, is to fit the style of the table to the style of the food and the service. Staff with t-shirts should never put food onto tables laid with starched tablecloths, for one thing is simply laughing at another. But those same staff must present you with a decent napkin, and not the sort of measly rag which so many Parisian brasseries make do with.

BISTROS DO NOT NEED TABLECLOTHS, but restaurants do. Cafés should use wood or glass or paper as a tabletop. I think unfolding a napkin into a customer's lap is a foolish affectation which I would be glad to see the end of, and I see no reason why so many restaurants still practice it. Would the waiter tuck a napkin into a customer's collar? Not in a million years. Why, then, should it be considered proper to unfold a napkin and drape it on a customer's lap?

The issue of tableware is, I think, essentially simple. If you use white tableware, then it acts as a frame for the colour of the food which is placed on it. If you use coloured tableware – especially tableware with vivid shades of red and blue – then you will lose the impact which the colour of the food offers against the background of a white plate.

But, used carefully and considerately, coloured tableware can have a place, especially if used with food which is white or pale in colour, when the plate provides the colour contrast.

Glassware should be serious, and not ridiculous. Huge balloons which wine lovers would never even use at home look foolish on a table, where modest glasses such as the ISO wine tasters glasses look appropriate. Whatever you do, avoid ostentation. Flashy glasses also cost a lot of money, and every time a waiter drops one, your heart will sink. So don't spend any more money than you need to.

Table spacing in a restaurant is an awkward problem, and once again it can only be solved by finding the right solution for the right space.

Hugger-mugger tables in a bistro actually create the sort of feel you want in that sort of space. In a formal restaurant, you must space the tables far enough apart so that people do not feel they can be overheard – if you have a business clientele, this is very important. In a café, benches can be not merely the cheapest solution, but also the best.

CHAIRS SHOULD ALWAYS BE COMFORTABLE, and this consideration must not be sacrificed in favour of design. Remember, people may well spend much longer sitting in a restaurant seat than in any other seat they occupy, so comfort, and marrying a chair of the correct height with the table, is of major importance.

Flowers can be one of the most striking and important decorations in any restaurant, and they should make their impact either by extreme simplicity – a single stem in a slender vase – or by being wildly effusive. They should never be too high – people need to see each other across a table – and they should not be too aromatic, for the aromas get in the way of the scents of the wine and the smells of the food. Once again, consider the overall impact in the context of the room, and marry the correct detail to the overall picture.

This, indeed, is the ultimate aim of design. Does the room suggest comfort, efficiency, liveliness and culture? Or does it look like an overdressed piece of domestic Colefax & Fowler let loose and on the rampage? The food must have its signature. So must the design, and original, inventive thinking is the best answer.

Lighting

Lighting is a difficulty for any restaurateur, a major difficulty.
Get it wrong – light tables from above, thereby casting shadows on people's faces as they talk and eat – and you will find yourself with an

empty restaurant, for downlighting is unflattering, and people do not go to restaurants to look less than their best.

Light the room too brightly, and everyone suddenly feels not only that the restaurant is a stage, but that they themselves are centre-stage, and exposed. Vulnerable. Many of your customers will not come back a second time.

GET IT RIGHT – have centred, localised lighting which can be controlled to suit the time of day and evening – and people immediately feel welcome and secure, comfortable.

Lighting is important in every restaurant, for along with greeting and music, it sets the mood. Lighting is part of the embrace of the restaurant experience, and must be judged to suit the room.

A wood panelled room with a low ceiling needs soft, golden, localised lighting. A great big barn with long tables can have overhead lighting far up at the ceiling and still work perfectly.

The main point here is to consider this subject very importantly, for it has a major influence on whether or not a room will work successfully. And be aware of the practicalities: lights on a table are a nuisance when it comes to serving food, even the simple candle in a bottle. Halogen lights are softer and more flattering to the customer. A room which is too dark is even more of a disaster than a room which is too bright. People need to be able to see the food, and to see each other. That is what dinner is all about.

Create Fashion, don't follow it

Every great restaurateur is always ahead of the fashion of the day, and one step ahead of the fashionable posse of the day. The great inventors and creators of the restaurant business never copy anyone, and they never follow trends. They invent trends, and by doing so, they attract the fashionable crowd who want to be where the action is.

The great restaurateurs, therefore, never stand still. Their work and their life is a constant procession of re-inventions of their style, their métier and their ambition. Ideally, the restaurateur who is running a successful restaurant should always be asking one simple question: "What's next?"

But great restaurateurs never do anything just to be fashionable. They do things right and, in so doing, they make them fashionable. There is nothing sadder than someone collecting all the bits and pieces that allegedly comprise the fashionable elements of the day, only to open their doors and discover that the fashion has already changed, and they have been left behind even before they started.
You can set your face against fashion, of course, and stand still in some sort of trattoria or gentleman's club style of a place. But, even here, you must still tweak and refine and reconsider, or else the restaurant will be dead on its feet.

You may have a regular clientele, who like things the way they are, but what you will not have are the customers looking for something new, and in every business – and especially in the world of restaurateuring – it is the customers you do not have who should concern you.

Restaurants, as places where we can see and be seen, are inextricably bound up with fashion. Sometimes, the fashion element is largely all they offer, but any good restaurateur should want to be considered amongst the movers and shakers of the modern age, simply because it shows that you are conscious of the contemporary culture, and thereby ready to play your part in it.

RESTAURANTS ABSORB AND REFLECT OUR CULTURE,
and the restaurant which claims to want no part of the modern society in which it operates is a sad place indeed.
Too many ethnic restaurants operate like this, and it is always to their detriment.

THE DETAILS

How to write a book

Every good cook should want to write a book. You should be confident enough that your work merits an audience beyond those for whom you can cook in the restaurant, and be confident enough that your voice is distinctive enough and different enough to be able to contribute something to the culinary culture.

Unfortunately, some chefs believe that the purpose of cookery books is to further flatter their already inflated egos. And, so, they produce books which are little other than exercises in vanity, and what they do in these books is nothing more than to spell out the menu dishes which they serve in the restaurant, and illustrate them with pointless, glossy photographs.

THESE BOOKS ARE A WASTE OF TREES.

Cookery books are only worthwhile if they have a true voice. The great cookery editor, Jill Norman, once defined a good book in this way: "I always felt there had to be a voice, you had to hear that someone was trying to say something, and not just put down a bunch of recipes. I wanted background and history and culture and attitudes, a feeling that someone had considered what they were doing, or would say quite openly that they were trying something out, or that they wondered about this".

Just as there must be a signature in your cooking in order to make it truly worthwhile, so there must be a signature voice striving to make sense of everything if you want to write a book. Recipes by themselves, particularly complex, cheffy recipes which are beyond the skill and pocket of domestic cooks, are a waste of time for everyone concerned.

We have spoken at length in this book about the culture of cookery, and the need to understand it at every level. Writing a book should, for a cook, be a crystallisation and codification of all that thought and inquiry.

BEING A CUSTOMER

THIS BOOK HAS BEEN ALL ABOUT A RESTAURATEUR'S RESPONSIBILITIES to his customers, and staff. But customers have responsibilities to restaurants, and these rules of behaviour and propriety are vital, if the relationship between customer and restaurateur is to enjoyed to the maximum.

TURN UP ON TIME

People who would never dream of being late for a domestic engagement often think there is nothing wrong with being half an hour late for a booking. This can cause major headaches for a restaurant, for it throws the planning and timing of the evening into disarray. It is extremely rude to be late for a booking, and even more rude, if there is good reason for being late, not to call the restaurant and alert them to the fact that you have been delayed.

STAY SOBER

Drunks are the most boring, annoying people on the planet. Yet, once again, people who would never dream of getting drunk if in a friend's house, often reckon they have carte blanche to get legless when in a restaurant. This is true largely of business suits, and groups out for a weekend night. Everyone likes people to have a good time, and restaurants make money from selling wine, but drunks are passé.

COMPLAIN POLITELY

If something is wrong, just bring it to the restaurateur's attention, and they will deal with it in an appropriate manner. If a slug gets in the lettuce, it's no big deal, just an oversight, and it does not entitle you to behave like a bear with a sore paw.

SAY THANK YOU

If something is really good in a restaurant, then say so. The performers – the cook, the restaurateur, the waiting staff – all love praise and applause, and most likely they deserve it.

THE TOTAL RESTAURANT

Final thoughts

I only read the testimonies of the restaurateurs, which follow in the appendix, after this book was almost completed, and I was astonished by the common currency which they and the text have mined.

The problems, challenges and delights of the restaurant business are the same, whether you are the chef, the restaurateur, the waiter, the plongeur, or the writer and critic sitting at the table, wondering if the restaurant is as good as it could be, wondering if it could achieve more, and more perfectly realise its ambitions.

Similarly, it does not matter what country you are discussing when you address the necessary strategies for success in the restaurant business. The elements of the restaurant entertainment – the vision, the creativity, the cooking, the consistency, the pressure, the production, the passion, the people – are the same throughout the world, irrespective of whether the restaurant is a twenty-two seater on a remote island, or a knock-'em-dead New York mega-production, with scores of staff and hundreds of punters.

Years ago, I gave a talk to a student group which dealt with the idea of the Total Restaurant. What was the Total Restaurant? It was a place, in my imaginings, where everyone got what they wanted out of the production. The restaurateur loved his job and made decent money. The chefs got a thrill out of their work, and produced gorgeous food, which the staff felt privileged to serve, to delighted customers who relished the atmosphere and swooned over the deliciousness of the food as they drank well-chosen, characterful wines and praised the good things of life.

And restaurants are one of the good things of life, one of the good entertainments, like music, books, movies, and at their best they take all the respective crafts of the business and fuse them into an intoxicating work of art.

THAT IS THE TOTAL RESTAURANT, SUBLIME AND BEAUTIFUL.

PERFECTION & POETRY

"...THE TRUE GOURMET, LIKE THE TRUE
ARTIST, IS ONE OF THE UNHAPPIEST
CREATURES EXISTENT.
HIS TROUBLE COMES FROM SO SELDOM
FINDING WHAT HE CONSTANTLY SEEKS:

PERFECTION"

Ludwig Bemelmans

"THERE IS POETRY
IN THE FAT FINGERS OF COOKS"

Nicolas Freeling

APPENDICES

APPENDIX 1

A DAY IN THE LIFE

Roly's Bistro, Dublin

The following piece appeared in 1994, in The Irish Times, and was an attempt to describe the controlled mayhem which is what a busy restaurant is all about.

Roly's Bistro has been one of the great success stories of modern Irish restaurant history. The three main characters – front of house man Roly Saul, chef Colin O'Daly and figures man John O'Sullivan – offer a brilliant combination of talents which have made the restaurant work, but what should be borne in mind is the fact that none of them previously worked in an operation like Roly's, which is an up-market room with high quality food at extremely keen prices.
Roly Saul had previously run a small restaurant in suburban Dun Laoghaire. Colin O'Daly had won stars and garlands for very complex, cheffy food served at high prices, whilst John O'Sullivan had cut his teeth on large scale, high volume restaurants. For all three, Roly's was a leap into the unknown, at a time when Dublin's economy was still rather fragile. Their bravery in opening Roly's found its reward from day one, and the restaurant would nowadays be running at full capacity for more than 90% of the time.

EIGHT-THIRTY ON A FRIDAY MORNING and Colin O'Daly, in crisp clean chef's-whites, is already about his business in Roly's Bistro. "Sleep is like rat poison", he says. "After a while you get immune to it". Mr O'Daly is taking to this poison rather well. Any possible bitterness from lack of sleep must surely be leavened by the fact that the success of Roly's Bistro, in the two years since it opened, is sweet as honey from the hive.
That success has been built on a fundamentally simple principle. It must be possible, reckoned Roly Saul, John O'Sullivan and Colin O'Daly, the three partners behind the Bistro, to combine volume,

value and good food. Put them together and you hit the ground running, and then build up speed.

But whilst principles are fine, it is in the day-to-day practice that success is made to endure. During the course of a day observing the entire operation of Roly's Bistro at work, I was struck by the fact that what Mr O'Daly calls "The octopus - it has arms all over the place" operates efficiently due to the interplay of the principal characters - Colin O'Daly, Roly Saul and John O'Sullivan - with the secondary characters - John the hatch man and John the floor manager upstairs, Gerry and James down in the basement kitchen; Jean Michel and John the principal chefs; Joyce and the rest of the squad of girls who work the floor.

"We're like John Rocha a bit", said Mr O'Daly. 'You go from a corner shop to a department store, but you keep the service and the quality of a corner shop, and you keep your own style".

BY THE TIME ROLY SAUL ARRIVES, followed shortly afterwards by John O'Sullivan, the basic preparations of the day are in full, quiet swing. The prawns - for the day's special of Fricassée of Dublin Bay Prawns with Vanilla Sauce - are being shelled, one by one. The cranberries are being sunk into the game pies and the pastry helmets neatly ringed around their tops. The vast volumes of broccoli are being par-cooked.

The lunch menu is a clever assertion of achievable cooking. There are five starters, two of which are soups. The half dozen main courses are Roasted Leg of Lamb, the Game Pies, Chicken Niçoise, Salmon Trout with a Fennel and Saffron Sauce, a Smoked Fish Cake and a Crêpe stuffed with Spinach, Oyster Mushrooms, Swiss Cheese and Sesame Seeds as the vegetarian choice.

This balance between dishes shows the influence of John O'Sullivan. Mr O'Sullivan, whose previous restaurants include Rafters in Rathmines and the original Blakes in Stillorgan, is an obsessive figures man. Shortly after his arrival, his wife brings in the print-outs of the previous day: every cutlet and caramel can be accounted for, the consumption of every bottle of Sancerre and glass of Smithwicks is revealed.

For Mr O'Sullivan, the matter is simple: you give people what they want. If there is something they don't want, they won't order it. Everything is standing up well, however, which creates a problem for the planned menu change in a week or so. If everything is shifting, then what can you replace? They will sort it out at the weekly management meeting on Tuesday.

BY MID-MORNING, the 'phone has commenced its mantric persistence. "Hello, Roly's, may-I-help-you?" and then the book is lifted and consulted, the names and 'numbers taken, the floor plans are opened and the names committed. It is here, perhaps, that we see one of the most remarkable features of Roly's: Mr Saul's Seating Situations.

Roly Saul is a peerless people-handler. He is a restaurant critic's nightmare, for he cannot forget a face and one's chances of sliding in here anonymously are almost zilch. He combines efficiency with the correct degree of professional nonchalance and command. "Mr Cassidy, sir, are you well?". "Good afternoon, welcome". "Would you like to come with me?". Whether those pushing the swing doors are celebs or ordinary decent folk, Mr Saul's words of welcome are one of the vital ingredients of Roly's Bistro.

But just as vital is his ability to play "3-D chess". This mind-boggling concept is the name Mr Saul gives to the business of who sits where. If you have a super-keenly priced lunch - and at £9.50 plus 10% service Roly's is a steal - then you need a large volume of customers at all times. Fall down on this bit and your kitchen staff will be becalmed, your floor staff bored, and you will be quickly bankrupt.

Mr Saul plays 3-D chess by knowing who is where at any and all of the many tables in Roly's at any given time of the day. If there is a cancellation or a no-show, then he must fill the table with folk who turn up with no reservation. If he knows that some customers will eat early and be gone, then he can sell the table twice in an evening. If he screws up, then the consequences don't bear thinking about. If he gets every-thing right, then he keeps this extraordinary edifice ticking over at maximum speed.

BY LATE MORNING, the wine delivery is being tucked away, the floor staff are arriving. In all, about 50 people are employed in Roly's, a business the size of a small factory. "It's like factory management here", says Mr O'Daly, hopping from floor to floor as the kitchens are assembled after their scrub-down, as the deliveries are checked in, "except we're all on the factory floor".

Mr O'Daly's ability to coin an aphorism is as sharp as his skills in the kitchen. In the success story of Roly's, his chameleon change from highly-wrought, individualised cooking to barnstorming brasserie master-minding has been indispensable. I thought, when he got the job, that Roly's had got the wrong man. After many visits to the Bistro, I relish eating those mistaken words every bit as much as I relish eating his food.

What Mr O'Daly does, aside from cooking and consulting, is to direct and inspire his staff. He has not traded in his sense of correctness, his devotion to his work, in favour of compromise and cop-out. In the cruel world of the professional restaurant, where chefs can find their vision and ambition crushed, Mr O'Daly continues to be excited, con-tinues to enjoy the whole business of cooking. His staff, fortunate for them, get this lesson for free.

ON A STANDARD FRIDAY LUNCHTIME, the restaurant will serve 'round about 150 covers. People begin to come through the doors about twenty minutes after twelve. In the kitchens on both the ground and first floors, the roasted legs of lamb are wrapped in foil after they are taken out of the roasting pans. The great trays of potato gratin bubble like so much hot lava as they are lifted out. The yellow dockets with the orders scribbled on them begin to arrive and to be posted above the hatches, where they flutter in the heat.

Even before the punters really begin to hit the seats, Colin O'Daly is bouncing up and down on his toes in the kitchen, eager for engagement. Downstairs, Jean Michel Poutot, by contrast, is cool, unfazed. Anyone who has ever worked in a kitchen knows this time well: the last breath of normal time before the assault is complete. There is the last chance to check things, the last chance for the plongeurs, with their ubiquitous pasty-complexions (I was one once - I had that complexion) to stack plates, check crockery, the last chance for the floor staff to see things are aligned correctly.

THEN, SUDDENLY, WE ARE IN THE INFERNO. IT IS ABOUT 12.45. The noise is shocking, the language between the staff incomprehensible: "How many prawns?". "4 prawns. There's 7 on it". The kitchen has been transformed into an ice hockey game, the blur of movement, the astonishing violence of speed, the roar of energy. Except that, here, no one bumps into anyone else. The choreography of a good kitchen is a thing of beauty. Intuitive, understood, startlingly efficient, and everything is accomplished in double-quick time.

Outside, the contrast is sublime. A few yards from the ice hockey game, we have an afternoon at Glyndebourne. This is the great secret, and the great truth, of restaurants. Without the maelstrom of the kitchen, with its pumping adrenaline and its hyperventilating staff, you cannot have the concordance of the dining room, with its relaxed customers and its ordered calmness. Without the speed and commitment of the kitchen, we cannot abdicate our cares to another time, shed our responsibilities for a while.

Friday afternoon, the October sunlight dithering through the blinds and, with work for the week almost done, you can smell the craving for this womb of greetings and g'n'ts, feel the hunger for that first sip of cool white wine with a plate of stuffed mussels. Jowls are quickly busy with chewing and conversation, in this singularly elegant dining room.

In the kitchen nobody walks, everybody runs, whilst Mark Ryan literally slides across the floor on his clogs. Joe the plongeur scrambles to the sink to clean up a new batch of pans. The noise. "Would you quit socialising over there for fuck's sake". "Very hot plate". "John, how's 22?". I realise, standing there as all this goes on, that my heart-beat has increased dramatically. "Joe, I need a pan please". "I don't wanna hear you don't know. Get me some flat leaf parsley". The staff slake their thirsts with pint glasses of orange squash. The puddings and parfaits begin to go out, then coffees. "That's okay Colin". "Are we over the hill?". "We're on the home stretch".

It has taken forty minutes. The tickertape of yellow dockets has dwindled from over the hatch, and migrated over to where James is doing desserts. At eight minutes past two there is only one docket left, but then a late party arrives: "2 pie, 2 fish, a prawns, and a lamb". In the dining room, the plink and plash of celebrating glasses is dwarfed by chatter super-charged with wine. By 2.45, the dining room upstairs is still largely full. Many of the punters are women, in small groups, in large groups, their behaviour more clubbale than the more-serious tables of businessmen.

Mr O'Daly, having worried his way through lunch, changes out of his whites and has lunch with Mr O'Sullivan and Mr Saul.

BY 7.30, THE FINAL LUNCH PARTY HAS JUST LEFT - "We'll go to Kitty O'Shea's!. Ah no, I can't. Go on, come on, come on. Aah, one then" - and the staff have returned everything to pristine perfection. Everything which has been done at lunchtime will now be done all over again, except there will be another 250 people involved, 250 people for whom the staff must perform as if this is opening night.

During her break, Joyce has been to see Keanu Reeves in "Speed". "Yeah, great", she says. "Great f.x.". "Keanu looks just like Colin", I say. "Chef's better looking", says Joyce.

Chef doesn't laugh. He has a single party of 36 French tourists to worry about. "Don't go 'til you're ready", he shouts into Mark and the others in the ground floor kitchen. "I want bam, bam, bam. I'd rather wait five minutes and have it right". The 36 French is not the problem. It is the party of 26 who will settle into their seats 25 minutes after they leave which is causing anxiety.

The discipline of planning a combination like this is terrifying. The ideal is to get 36 main courses out as close to simultaneous as possible. To do this, what each diner has ordered is marked on the table plans, so the right waitress takes the right order to the right person and does not have to ask who ordered what.

"Right lads, we're going to go", shouts Mark Ryan, working the evening shift downstairs. Suddenly, the kitchen is a madhouse. "1 more after this". "What's next Ronny?". "3 turbot, 1 beef". The heat level ascends to boiling, sweat breaks out on everybody's face. The turbot fillets are placed gently on their beds of spinach, then a sun-dried tomato and pistou vinaigrette is danced around the plate, a dice of tomato scattered on. One after another, after another. The concern shown for the arrangement of food on each plate is amazing. There is a huddle as the veg is readied: colcannon, green beans, carrot purée. The floor staff wait with operating theatre expressions, then grab plates and chase away quick as teenagers who have just been given the car keys.

DOWNSTAIRS, THEY ARE ALREADY INTO TOMORROW. The young trainee is getting a lesson in how to peel an onion. Later, he will get a lesson in how to cut up a cauliflower. The beef, lamb and chicken stocks simmer away in the corner, in the surreal calm.

Nanci Griffith and the Chinese Circus have given them a hard time. "We got hammered at 6 o'clock. Going on to the Point and the RDS. The venison is good. You do get feedback, that's nice. They like it. It's wild", says John the floor manager. "You do get a sixth sense in this business. I try to teach them to anticipate people's needs, tell them to treat people the way they want to be treated when they go out".

The character of Roly's Bistro comes into its best at this time of evening, I think. It's not truly a bistro, of course, but a brasserie, and the low lights and chatter of early evening seem to me to be its best companions. Mr O'Daly does a quick tour of the tables at 8.30, hand-shakes and how-are-you's?. Roly Saul is downstairs, as usual, standing at his podium, welcoming the individuals who quickly congress into groups: "I'm Mary. How are you. A sherry".

Dinner is more difficult than lunch, for every system in the kitchen must work side by side. The quenelles of liver mousse are being prepared as the blow-torch caramelises the tops of the crème brûlées. An eye must be kept on the lamb's liver and kidney at the same time as the fillets of beef.

This planning - the orchestration of diners to their tables, the taking and posting of orders, the timing of starters, main courses and desserts, the checking and correction of orders - would stymie the most sophisticated computer imaginable. In Roly's Bistro, on Friday night, the orchestration is so seamless one might imagine Astaire had taught them how to move and Richard Strauss had scored the melody for the evening.

Maybe Astaire is the wrong comparison. The 36 French have been happily fed, and the tables they occupied cleared, cleaned and re-set in a matter - literally - of minutes. Mr Saul is beaming. "It's like Busby Berkeley", he says. Proud as punch. "Marvellous meal", says one man, departing with a handshake.

BY 9 O'CLOCK, the cacophony of voices from the tables is counterpointed by the quiet efficiency of the kitchens as they simply go about their business: John the hatch-man standing in judgment over every plate that goes out; Jean Michel easily marshaling every order; the waitresses drenching the coffee grounds with hot water; the wine orders flowing steadily from the bar downstairs; the youthful runners pegging up and down the stairs like yo-yo's. This calmness, of course, is right at the centre of the storm, for the place is buzzing.

Kitchens work by discipline, and intuition, for there is little dialogue other than barked orders. Everybody has to do what everybody has to do. Everybody understands that there are no second acts in restaurant history. There are only bankruptcies.

RESTAURATEUR'S TESTIMONIES

I asked some of the most successful and creative restaurateurs for a testimony about their feelings for the business. Some kept strictly to my request for a resumé of things they wish they had known when they started their careers, others diverged from the brief to offer wider thoughts and opinions.

MYRTLE ALLEN

Ballymaloe House
Shanagarry, County Cork

I suppose I was lucky that I didn't know anything except how to satisfy a gourmet husband and how to handle the products I had to hand, which I had enough experience to realise were superb. In 1964

I reckoned that the food I could put on our family table could be increased in volume without detracting from its quality and could not be worse than what was on offer in other restaurants in and around Cork.

Basically, I am thankful I did not know anything more than just that.

1. Have a realistic and straight forward approach, avoiding all pretentiousness.

2. In order to survive financially, cut waste, and not quality of food by buying cheaply. In fact, it is very hard to cut the price of a meal and make a living and serve good quality food. A tremendous amount of skill is involved in achieving the balance.

3. Buy in small quantities frequently, so that your food is always fresh.

4. Always pay attention to even the most stupid letters and criticisms, but, at the same time don't be over-influenced by them.

5. Be generous to your customers and taxi and bus drivers who bring them (but not to the point of paying commissions).

6. Have choices on your menu that will please different kinds of people.

7. Be constantly on guard against unexpected disasters – never for a minute relax your vigilance.

8. Don't use your imagination just for the sake of seeming imaginative.

9. Serve what you know you can cook well, use your own good sense, what you think is good and delicious. Then, keep your ears cocked for comments and adjust accordingly.

10. Keep hoping that you can continue to ignore all those wretched customers that look for swanky food, and hope that the critics are good enough to distinguish the difference between trendy, pretentious menus and the quality of food on the plate – one will eventually!

The other really important thing is, decor, ambiance and style – you either have it or you haven't, also don't cook just for restaurant critics!! And don't open a restaurant if you can't cook.

PASCAL BRADLEY

101 Talbot, Talbot Street, Dublin

1. If starting in the business, beware of your own naiveté.

2. Use a computer from the outset no matter how little you know of them – a friend will help you (we came to computers five and a half years too late).

3. Select staff who wish to make a career rather than money out of their work. (A brain is necessary in as many of your staff as possible – people who work "on automatic" with loads of experience are not always best).

4. Everyone is replaceable – mainly your Prima Donna head chef. In fact lose him today so that you can replace him/her as soon as possible.

5. Delegate as soon as possible in order to save yourself for the more important decisions (not seeing "the wood for the trees" can happen quickly).

6. Be as legal as possible as soon as possible in regard to your staff (There seems to be a current trend of head chefs roving around saying 'OK give me so many hundred pounds per week and don't put me on the books').

7. Avoid people who presume that a catering college education means that they know everything.

8. Treat all customers as you would a best friend visiting your home. (If they behave badly you can always throw them out or refuse to allow them back in the future). Your staff should behave the same way – when the customer is absolutely on your side I reckon you can get away with murder and be forgiven.

9. Try and start up where your business is needed rather where it's "trendy" to be.

10. A good review is worth thousands of pounds in advertising. But word of mouth is the very best advertising. Every new customer who comes in will pass the word to five to ten people if they like place. If they don't, thirty or forty people will hear about it.

FRANCIS BRENNAN
The Park Hotel, Kenmare, County Kerry

1. Be good humoured.
2. Cultivate a dislike of sport.
3. Have a good work ethic.
4. Be a mind reader.
5. Be well read.
6. Have good interpersonal skills.
7. Be an accountant!
8. Have good feet.
9. Enjoy company.
10. Honestly know your food and wine

DENIS COTTER
Café Paradiso
Western Road, Cork

1. Hire staff carefully – catering tends to be careless and abusive with staff. They need to fit in personally as well as be efficient, and to, ideally, understand and support the complex and unique nature of the restaurant.
2. Floor staff need to do that old Rose of Tralee thing – enjoy working with the (often very contrary but interesting) public. Above all, avoid those prone to arrogance and taking it all personally.
3. Feed the floor staff very well (not "staff food"). They should know the menu, not just memorise the written details of it.
4. Create a happy kitchen atmosphere. The best food is soul food and you can't cook it in anger, chaos or that sweaty, macho, it's-hell-in-here-but-we'll-get-the-job-done atmosphere so beloved of catering regiments. Ever notice that women don't cook like that? Food is a great karma carrier and customers pick it up even if they don't taste it.

5. Be aware that a restaurant is a medium in which people enjoy each other's company. It is not a stage for floor performance, nor an exhibition space for artistic displays of food arrangements.

6. Cynicism and marketeering always show. The only things that you can be truly confident about selling is something you'd love to buy. That's why the best restaurants are, in all their aspects, expressions of the people who create them.

7. Sensible budgeting is not the same as skimping. For example, if you're unsure of how many asparagus stalks to put on a dish, put an extra one on and charge enough. If the customer buys it they'll enjoy it. If they can't afford it, they certainly wouldn't have liked the mean version. It's crucial to remove the "value for money" obstacle. The customers can't enjoy their evening if their minds are constantly being distracted by the thought that they might be cheated.

8. However! Make a profit! It's bloody hard work and you will quickly become cynical if your only reward is spiritual. Forgetting about the bank balance is the surest way to retract on the fine promises you just made.

9. Put back in, in terms of dining room improvement, service improvement, menu changes etc. The place becomes the regular customers' as much as yours and they love to see it being maintained and improved.

10. Ignore all the above if you're an accountant thinking of setting up a restaurant as an investment.

JOHN DESMOND
Island Cottage Restaurant, Heir Island, County Cork

The following would be my 10 points in order to run a restaurant successfully. The order of the points is not relevant.

1. Have a very good background knowledge of the business you intend to run (education, training, experience, etc, especially experience in other types of similar businesses.)

2. Believe in what you are doing and look at the long term.

3. Know your strengths and weaknesses.

4. When starting your business keep your price below the competition and your quality above.

5. Always try to improve your business internally on an on-going basis.

6. Be consistent.

7. Raise your prices very slowly.

8. It is important to be able to say no.

9. Do not try to please everybody.

10. If you want to make a lot of money do not go into the restaurant business, buy a McDonald's franchise instead.

MAURA FOLEY

Packie's Restaurant
Kenmare, County Kerry

Passion: is natural, it cannot be bought, and it is like love.

Palate: to develop your palate, always try new tastes and keep up to date, and never serve food that you do not taste.

Persistence: you have got to be constant, it is no good if it is good today and bad tomorrow. One bad dinner loses 100 customers.

Food does not create a restaurant feel – this great, misused word, now often called ambience – and this is what it is all about; the perfect party is created, and it does not happen by chance. The lighting, the atmosphere, the service and finally the food are the factors which create it.

Do not dream of going into the restaurant business unless you feel it is your scene. You will not make a fortune, but, on the other hand, if you are flat broke it is the only way. Rent, Sweat and Perform: it is a performance every night, a new performance. Yesterday is dead, tomorrow is not relevant – it is the now: the people, the food, the service, the value, the everything. Does it come off? We may scream in the kitchen, and say, "They do not know" – but we will be poor chefs and restaurateurs tomorrow if this is our attitude.

We have got to do the impossible, give of oneself totally, and if it does not do, then apologise for our inadequacies.

The worst customer is the one whose dreams are higher than our performance.

It is a rough business and only for those who can stand the heat, take the pressure and stay in the cold.

Praise is nothing, criticism is far greater.

No matter how one tries one will not please everybody all the time.

One has to be able to live with one's limits, but always do your best.

In good restaurants there are no VIPs. All your customers are VIPs. This is the essence of a good restaurant. My grandmother said, in her grocery shop which is now Packie's, when a local squire thought he should be served before a local customer: "There is a crown on this man's shilling too!" Everybody that chooses to eat in one's restaurant is a special customer.

The restaurant business is a mad business for mad people, who sweat, worry, get carried away with themselves, but all is lost if they cannot laugh and retain a sense of humour. It is serious, but not the end of the world. When Colin O'Daly cooked in the restaurant of The Park Hotel, the girl in the wash-up used to stand and look at us and say: "You are all mad", and she was so objective in her observation, but love and passion are mad, there is no inbetween.

GERARD GALVIN

Drimcong House, Moycullen, County Galway

1. I wish I had had the courage and foresight to have taken more time with my family in the early days. Restaurateuring eats up families!

2. It is important to understand that financial reward is not the most

important facet of a serious career as a restaurateur. If one can have this basic view from the beginning rather than spending years resenting the toil for unexpectedly low income, life is more enjoyable.

3. Three essentials: the best accountant, best solicitor, best doctor.

4. Service not servility.

5. A lot is learned painfully, but learned!

6. Happy bosses, happy staff, happy customers.

7. Don't allow suppliers to insult food.

8. It is a mistake to presume that good food alone makes for good restaurants.

9. Spread bookings: the restaurant that allows all its customers to arrive at 8.30pm is courting disaster.

10. Encourage children, and thereby create the next generation of diners.

YOICHI HOASHI

Ayumi Ya Restaurant
Blackrock and Baggot Street, Dublin

1. Love the business of restaurant keeping, so respect the customer's choice of coming to your premises and enjoy seeing the customer so that he/she goes home happy to look forward to their next visit. This involves living for the business and severe commitment. Very often, the restaurant is almost an extension of the proprietor's personality in terms of food, ambience, service.

2. Marketing – know the market and know who you are catering to, then design your product (menu, premises, ambience, pricing, service, style etc etc).

3. Cooking and Service in equal importance.

4. Controls and management infrastructure are vital.

5. Train all staff to respect their work and be able to appreciate their

contribution they make. This has to be done by way of leading by example.

6. Administration – PAYE/PRSI, VAT, Wages records, accounts, staff records, cash and bank handling, must be taken care of.

7. Innovation, Promotion – use all these things to keep the restaurant product fresh and stimulating to the customer.

8. OR – looking after the regular customer over and above the general customers who also have to be looked after because they are your regular customers of tomorrow.

9. To be self critical at all times.

10. To be able to be the "Jack of all trades".

EUGENE McSWEENEY

Lacken House
Kilkenny, County Kilkenny

1. I wish I had known that customers would try to tell you how to run your business and how to cook.

2. I wish I had known that I would get no help from Bord Failte.

3. My first Bank Manager laughed at my idea of offering a restaurant in Kilkenny.

4. I wish I had known about the loss of so much personal time as an owner.

5. Avoid pushy salesmen.

6. Avoid pushy advertising people.

7. Be prepared for the vast amount of book work.

8. Murphy's Law.

9. When you run a restaurant you need to be very strong in mind and body, for the demands are great.

10. Be married to someone like Breda who had no training, but without her help and drive I would not have been successful.

LIZ MEE
The Elephant & Castle, Temple Bar, Dublin

1. You must give yourself totally to the business – you really have to sacrifice a personal life, particularly when you are trying to have some semblance of family life as well.

2. Consistency – it is vitally important to maintain consistency – it is something we emphasise all the time with staff. It is amazing the number of times customers comment on our consistency.

3. Never take no for an answer – we never accept that we cannot get something or that there is not some way around a problem – steely determination.

4. Be patient with staff – you will rarely have the perfect staff member so look to their positive points and hope to improve their bad ones. Some people take a lot of time and patience and it's incredibly good when they blossom.

5. Be loyal to suppliers and pay them on time, therefore when you need something in a hurry or at an odd time they will generally go out of their way to help.

6. Look after your regular customers and be particularly nice to customers with children. Children make very loyal customers.

7. Never make drastic changes to one's menu. We make minor changes twice a year and innovate on our specials. Certain customers have particular favourites and certain dishes may not have widespread appeal but have a few loyal fans. Specials must also suit the style of our restaurant – nothing must jar.

8. Things I wished I'd known:
– how much one lives in dreads of a visit from the Health Inspector – food is almost not food anymore but a dangerous product. This is a subject I could discourse endlessly on. Of course, we are very conscious of food safety, but...
– fear of being sued – I think I was an innocent up until the day we opened the restaurant – this has a real impact on how one runs a business and is a big worry.

– increasing bureaucracy – every year it gets worse and worse – more and more statistical reports to complete etc etc. When we first opened my brother helped us with accounts and tax but we have long had a full-time book keeper. We are busy enough to support this but for smaller businesses it must be a real worry.

9. Always offer a quality product – be conscious that people are spending hard-earned money. Always be kind and courteous. I go mad if customers are treated with disinterest. No matter how good the food in a restaurant is, if one is not properly treated a return visit is rarely made.

10. Despite everything, it's a most fascinating business.

HELEN MULLANE
& ARMEL WHYTE

Allo's Bar & Bistro, Listowel, County Kerry

1. Getting the right financial and accounting advice from the very beginning is the difference between a viable and non-viable business.

2. VAT is the killer. When calculating the food costing, don't forget to allow for VAT – even on a cup of coffee.

3. If you don't have time or the ability to do the daily book keeping, get your accountant to do them. Unfortunately there is heaps of paperwork. One spends a lot of time collecting taxes for an inefficient government.

4. It's easier to get advise from your "unfriendly" health inspector in the beginning, as they have the power to make you correct your "shortcuts" later when it will probably cost you a lot more money then and could affect your time and operating schedule. If you are operating from an older kitchen or on a lease situation where conditions are not ideal, then generally the inspector can be met half way. Do not get cranky with them, they are only doing their job.

5. Set up costs are frightening. Don't be put off. You have to spend

money to make money. Kitchen equipment can be bought second-hand or leased. If buying new, get a couple of quotes from various suppliers.

6. Market research is important. After all there is no point in offering your style of cooking if there is no demand.

7. It's a good idea to specialize. It gives you direction e.g. organic, seafood.

8. We find having a full drinks licence is good – more choice for the customer and better drinks sales.

9. Never ever sit back on your laurels. Just when you think you have everything going to your liking you get a problem that needs attention. Menus need constant changing if you have very regular customers. There is a huge variety of wines available – keep a check on your wine lists, adding new wines regularly from different suppliers. Don't be lazy and get one wine company to do your full list. Variety is the spice of life.

10. After all that, running your own restaurant is so rewarding and well worth all the effort, the late nights and hard work. Cooking gives us ultimate pleasure and serving food to a table of appreciating customers justifies the efforts. It's great fun.

ALAN O'REILLY

Morels Bistros
Glasthule and Leeson Street, Dublin

SOME PERSONAL THOUGHTS AND RAMBLINGS.

As you are well aware restaurants in general, are living breathing things that thrive on all kinds of emotions. Some are purely Chef de Patron driven, some consortium managed, some solely money making ventures hatched out between business men who reckon they can make a lot of money on a 'chicken breast'.

Some are run by media created paranoid schizophrenic paedimorphs who use them as a tool to feed their massive egos. Being a product of the catering school myself from an early age I found this 'dominating' and all too often suffocating. Going into business for myself I actually tried to change this: by trying to get away from the strict regimented party system in kitchens, to deliberately not taking on students from the College of Catering with City & Guilds examinations, to working with people who loved to taste, eat and enjoy cooking food. For these reasons extremely fresh food, meat, fish, game and vegetables (which so often sounds like a cliché!) is enough to create the high level of motivation that's required to run a restaurant on a daily basis.

The most important parts of the restaurant business is energy and inspiration. These are like the blood of the restaurant: it must flow to all parts like the blood in our own veins. Its energy has to run not just from the chef-food-kitchen, but right through the restaurant. The person who is the connection between chef and customer must be equally as charged energetically from the customer. All this must be done, but not in a condescending and highbrow fashion, as at the end of the day it should be a happy and enjoyable experience for the customer and not an intimidating or threatening one.

Looking back now, I feel all chefs should only become chefs when they develop their own intellect, as too many young chefs are influenced by all things not food, i.e. what they see as the attraction of fame and fortune. They don't always have the necessary passion and heart.

When you take all these emotional thoughts and frame them into a business it thus becomes a living breathing 'nightmare' to some people. All this with media pressure on some chefs, especially young ones, to change and develop the Irish food culture can lead to new heights in food, but unfortunately these heights are all too often the 'bland vertical architectural type' which may suit people with bland vertical architectural type palates.

Passion for food, tastes and cooking comes with life. Drive and unholy devotion are personal things to all cooks but kitchens (especially those in the eyes of the chicken businessmen) are predominately small, hot, cluttered places with sometimes up to ten human beings under strict time restraints to create their wares. A frightening scenario, but passion creates such things.

The restaurant business anyone can enter. It's not strictly licensed by the government which is not a bad thing. Unfortunately restaurants are serious businesses from a small company point of view and play by the same rules as large private companies such as Dunnes Stores in the eyes of the Revenue Commissioners and the Government. They suffer unfair and sometime crippling VAT rates that can drive even the best restaurants into the ground. So running a restaurant with good office and accountancy backup is an equally vital part of the restaurant business. All too often passionate cooks find themselves in deep financial difficulties by neglecting the financial part of their restaurant. This in turn leads to inferior quality produce, staff shortages, unhappy customers and inevitably the death of a restaurant.

Restaurants are a labour of love, I know that sounds clichéd but there is no other way to put it. One of the most satisfying things about it is the constant learning. The passionate cook , the brilliant, slick, suave Maitre d', the ego maniac, the chicken business man are all learning all the time, for better or for worse.

At the end of the day the most important thing is not to give preconceived notions of tastes, flavours, expectations and experiences to the customers and then to take them away. There is nothing worse than disappointing the receptive palate, being true to one's customer can only be achieved by being true to one's self.

keeper, banker, psychologist, researcher, sometimes nurse, buyer, and by the way, Chef! You can't do it all – I did. Before you begin, select one or two of the above, and perfect at least one!

7. A Thin Line: In hindsight, I was faced with a huge dilemma: to make real money or to make acceptable choices for me. Real money: a) pack in as many people as possible; b) do take home pizza; c) Franchise. It appeared to many that I kicked a gift horse in the mouth. A passion for food is costly, and way more rewarding than cash.

8. Wait Staff Abuse: I am convinced that wait staff should have a degree in psychology. It didn't happen frequently but enough times to convince me that people were sometimes prepared to act out abusive behaviour towards staff. Waiting on tables has low profile status, and is not really understood. People sometimes abused this service.

9. Menu Change: Rather than giving people what they want, I discovered that frequent menu change encouraged people to come to the restaurant more frequently. Organic produce will drive the kitchen in this direction also.

10. Close the restaurant, and take good breaks. This recharges the brain and inspires. Inspiration time is the soul of a good restaurant.

NICK PRICE
Nick's Warehouse
Hill Street, Belfast

1. To us running a restaurant is all about imposing our tastes on the general public, one has to be slightly arrogant about this as otherwise you get washed away in a tide of sameness.

2. The trick is to remember that you are in business to make money and whilst it may be a very "fun" idea to run a restaurant, it is no good offering fabulous food and selling it for less than it costs you to produce!!

3. Remember that people going out for a meal are usually there for an

BERNADETTE O'SHEA

**formerly of Truffles Restaurant
Sligo, County Sligo**

1. Shock Staff Situation: Hot from the U.S. – the home of great service – I find that there are no such standards of service in Ireland. It's up to the restaurant to groom its staff in a particular style, but this depends on a basic command of service – there was none.

To this day I still ask 'What has Bord Failte been doing all these years?' 'What was Cert and Fás at?' I was so lucky to find the people who came to work in Truffles. My demands were a shock to the system – it was hard work but they took it on and did so well.

2. Organic Luck: It was difficult to get a lot of the Mediterranean ingredients to the West, but the biggest surprise of all was my total conversion to locally grown organic produce. Better than any sunkissed product I had ever eaten. It changed everything. My menu responded to the availability of produce and was determined not by me, but availability and the season, the climate, the earth, the farmer

3. Wine Weary Boys! – Revelations: Another shock! The revelatio that wine salesmen, with just one exception, were the most uned cated about their "product", most disorganized, most disrupti (appeared at the most unacceptable of hours) and proved to be least capable of undoing their mistakes. Has anyone really through to the wine companies yet? I still shudder when I thinl them.

4. No Loot: The pressure of being under-financed in the begir robbed too much time from my life, forcing me to work all the l God sent. I should have had a better business plan. Next time!

5. People Power: I never thought for a moment that throu cooking I would get to know so many wonderful people. In hir it's the most unprepared for gift. Glowing, warming, loving ence of people that made Truffles so renowned. Pure people p

6. Real Role Play: I was manager, stock keeper, employe

occasion, a night out, so it has to be always special, no matter how hung over you are feeling, the show must go on, even if all the power fails and you have an all-electric kitchen – like last Friday night!!

4. Realise at the outset that it's impossible to please all the people all of the time, smile and do your best, you are human too.

5. If someone complains... grovel, then grovel some more.

Don't try and justify, no matter how good your excuse, they aren't usually interested.

We have only ever torn up someone's bill and asked them to leave once. It was worth it just to see the stunned expression on their faces, but as a business practice it's not recommended.

6. Attention to detail. It's the little things that matter. Staff must be constantly reminded, cajoled, kicked and generally encouraged to get it right.

7. After eighteen years in the business we are quite convinced that there are customers who just go out to give a restaurant a hard time. Grit your teeth and be so revoltingly pleasant that after their third visit you have them eating out of your hand.

8. Wine lists.

Don't let the wine merchant do it unless he is as arrogant as you are. The same rule applies to wine merchants as apply to restaurateurs. Take an interest, get knowledgeable and if you don't know anything about it, consult someone whose list you respect. They will either be flattered or tell you to get stuffed.

9. You or your partner must be able to do every job in the place, so you are not at the mercy of key staff. It's also useful to have a mechanical bent in the firm to be able to fix the cooker when it breaks in the middle of service and the repair man can't get to you for two days.

10. Don't call your restaurant by your own name if you ever want to sell it. Why would Jack want to buy Nick's Restaurant anyway.

11. Don't chop and change your opening hours.

It confuses the hell out of people. i.e. we originally said we were not going to open at night, a policy we reversed after one year. Now, seven year's later, people still think we don't open at night.

BIBLIOGRAPHY

● Bemelmans, Ludwig. *La Bonne Table.*
New York: Godine, 1989

● Dorf, Martin. *Restaurants That Work.*
New York: Whitney Library of Design, 1992

● Freeling, Nicolas. *The Kitchen Book/The Cook Book.*
London: Andre Deutsch, 1991

● Galvin, Gerard. *The Drimcong Food Affair.*
Galway: MacDonald, 1992

● Goldman, William. *Adventures in the Screen Trade.*
London: MacDonald & Co., 1984

● McKenna, Sally and John.
The Bridgestone Irish Food Guide.
Durrus: Estragon Press, 1991, 1993, 1996.

The Bridgestone 100 Best Restaurants in Ireland.
Durrus: Estragon Press, 1992-1998

The Bridgestone 100 Best Places to Stay in Ireland.
Durrus: Estragon Press, 1992-1998

The Bridgestone Dublin Food Guide.
Durrus: Estragon Press, 1997

● Waters, Alice. *The Chez Panisse Menu Cookbook.*
New York: Random House, 1982